AF673211

India Design Book

2018-19

Confederation of Indian Industry

First published in India in 2019 by HarperCollins Publishers
A-75, Sector 57, Noida, Uttar Pradesh 201301, India
www.harpercollins.co.in

2 4 6 8 10 9 7 5 3 1

Copyright © (2019) Confederation of Indian Industry (CII). All rights reserved.

ISBN: 9789353574611

The views and opinions expressed in this book are the author's own and the facts are as reported by them, and the publishers are not in any way liable for the same.

CII asserts the moral right to be identified as the author of this work.

Design by Haitenlo Semy

Printed and bound at Replika Press Pvt. Ltd

This book is produced from independently certified FSC® paper to ensure responsible forest management.

Copyright © (2019) Confederation of Indian Industry (CII). All rights reserved.

Without limiting the rights under the copyright reserved, this publication or any part of it may not be translated, reproduced, stored, transmitted in any form (electronic, mechanical, photocopying, audio recording or otherwise) or circulated in any binding or cover other than the cover in which it is currently published, without the prior written permission of CII.

All information, ideas, views, opinions, estimates, advice, suggestions, recommendations (hereinafter 'content') in this publication should not be understood as professional advice in any manner or interpreted as policies, objectives, opinions or suggestions of CII. Readers are advised to use their discretion and seek professional advice before taking any action or decision, based on the contents of this publication. The content in this publication has been obtained or derived from sources believed by CII to be reliable but CII does not represent this information to be accurate or complete. CII does not assume any responsibility and disclaims any liability for any loss, damages, caused due to any reason whatsoever, towards any person (natural or legal) who uses this publication.

This publication cannot be sold for consideration, within or outside India, without express written permission of CII. Violation of this con–dition of sale will lead to criminal and civil prosecution.

Published by Confederation of Indian Industry (CII), The Mantosh Sondhi Centre; 23, Institutional Area, Lodi Road, New Delhi 110003, India, Tel: +91-11-24629994-7, Fax: +91-11-24626149; Email: info@cii.in; Web: www.cii.in

CONTENTS

Foreword

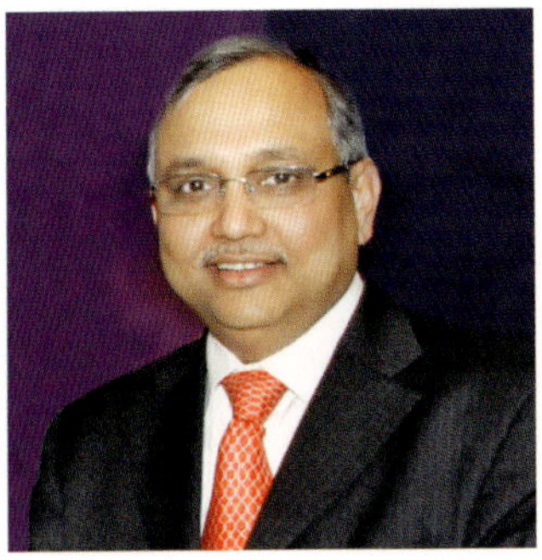

Chandrajit Banerjee

Director General, Confederation of Indian Industry

For the last 18 years, the Confederation of Indian Industry (CII) has been working towards strengthening the economy and society by demonstrating and promoting the vital role of design in making businesses more competitive and public services more effective.

CII initiated various programs, supported several initiatives and has achieved significant success in spearheading the national design direction and developing design excellence. To document and present the state of design in India, we had initiated the CII Design Year Book in 2014. It is the only annual book in the country that presents contemporary work from myriad design disciplines, showcases innovative solutions and vital advancements and covers the key areas where design has left its mark, by presenting case studies of Indian products and services.

As the Indian industry grows, the current edition of the book reconfirms the critical role that design plays in envisioning new products, services and communications. This book would be a very useful tool for readers in their activities in advancement of competitive development.

Message

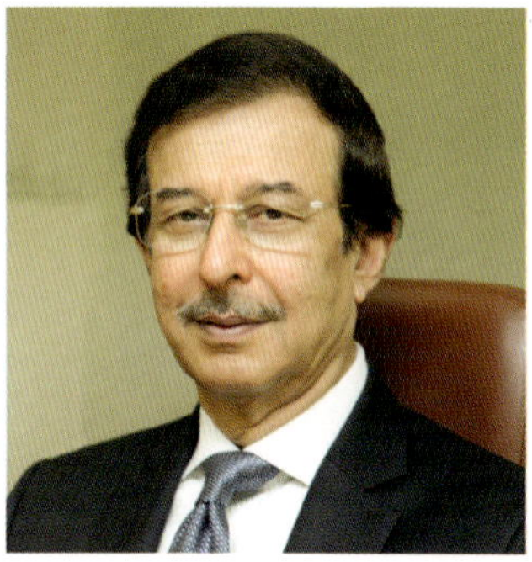

Deep Kapuria

Chairman, CII National Committee on Design

Chairman, The Hi-Tech Gears Ltd.

Design is at a high impetus of national agenda for many countries and therefore, to foster a competitive growth around the world, there is an emphasis on strategic use of design. Many governments are developing and implementing design policies and promotion programs, not only to boost their industry and business competitiveness, but also to increase awareness of design in public lives, even to solve complex social issues such as public health systems, crime abatement, energy saving, geriatric needs, and so on.

Design is also an integral part of innovation, essential for sustainability of the nation. Any investment on design reflects positively and enhances the competitiveness and improves the market reach of the industries. Several studies have shown a strong interrelationship between national competitiveness and design. The CII National Committee on Design is resolute in its endeavour to foster design led innovation towards a robust economy.

The CII *India Design Book* is an assorted collection of product designs and case-studies that makes it an ultimate resource to the Indian industry. Aimed specifically at businesses, manufacturers, institutions, designers and students, it could be an awe-inspiring repository of inspiring information on today's trends and future directions, making it a must-have possession.

The book features contributions from the leading design consultants and design led companies, whose experiences and insights would prove invaluable to many. It unfolds many evocative stories of symbiosis between design and manufacturing. I have no doubt that this edition showcasing delated case-study of product/service design of the book will serve as a formal source of reference for design excellence in India.

On behalf of the CII National Committee on Design, we are honoured to present this publication to the practitioners and connoisseurs of good design. I am sure that the work curated and showcased in these pages would go a long way in igniting readers' appreciation for design. I hope that you will enjoy learning about many aspects related to design and bestow its significance to support dynamic and progressive industry sector.

In closing, I would like to thank wholeheartedly all the contributors for their engagement as well as the CII team that has been instrumental in the book's publication.

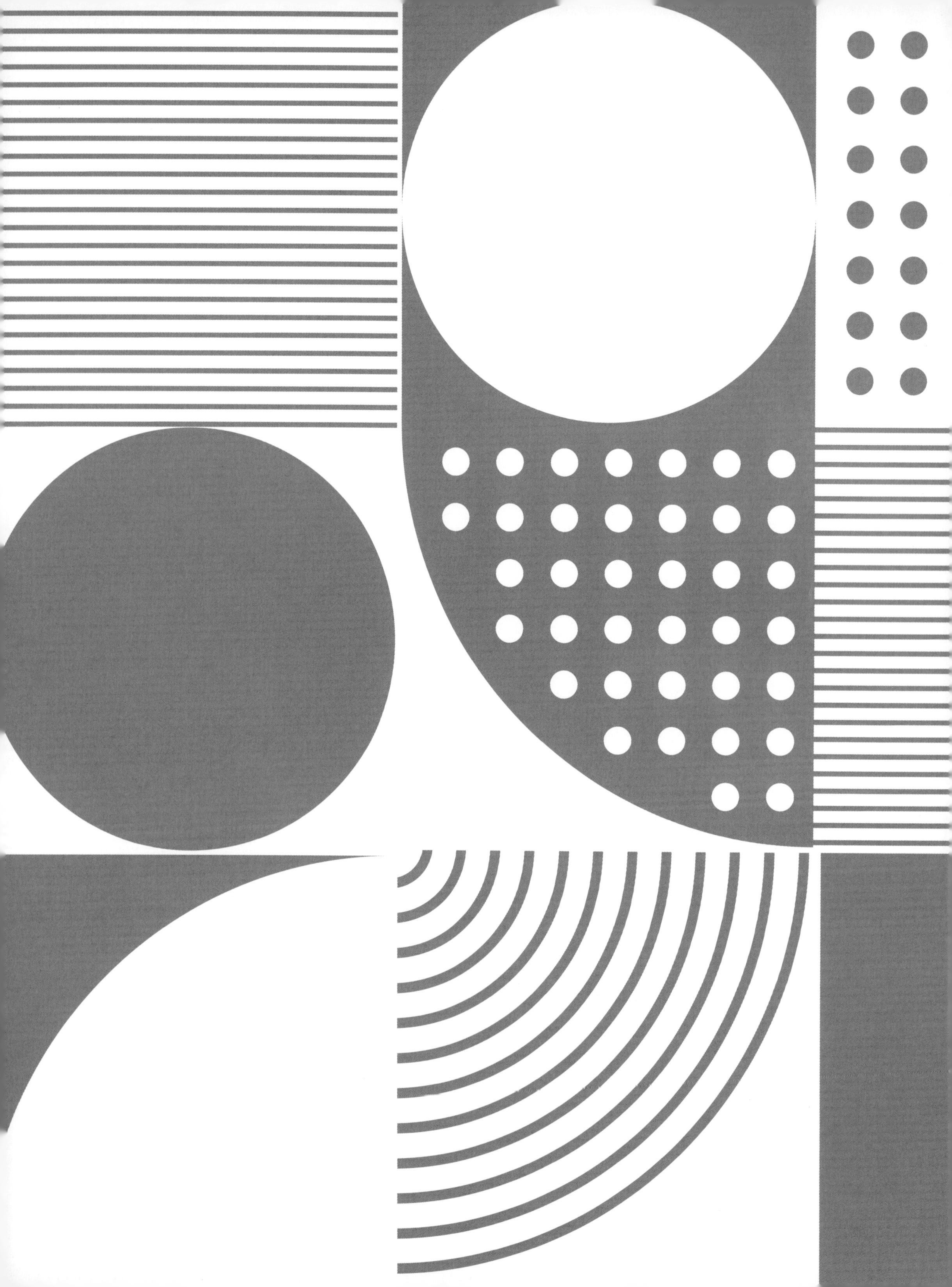

INDUSTRIAL DESIGN

CARBONADO

Carbonado

The World's First Hybrid Techpack

CONTACT INFORMATION

Company Name: BPLUGD IOT Pvt Ltd

Company Address: #101, A wing, Carlton Towers, HAL II Stage, Kodigalli, Bangalore-560008

Name of Contact Person: Pradeep Reddy

Contact Number: +91 9036944777

Email Address: pradeep@bplugd.com

Website URL: www.bplugd.com

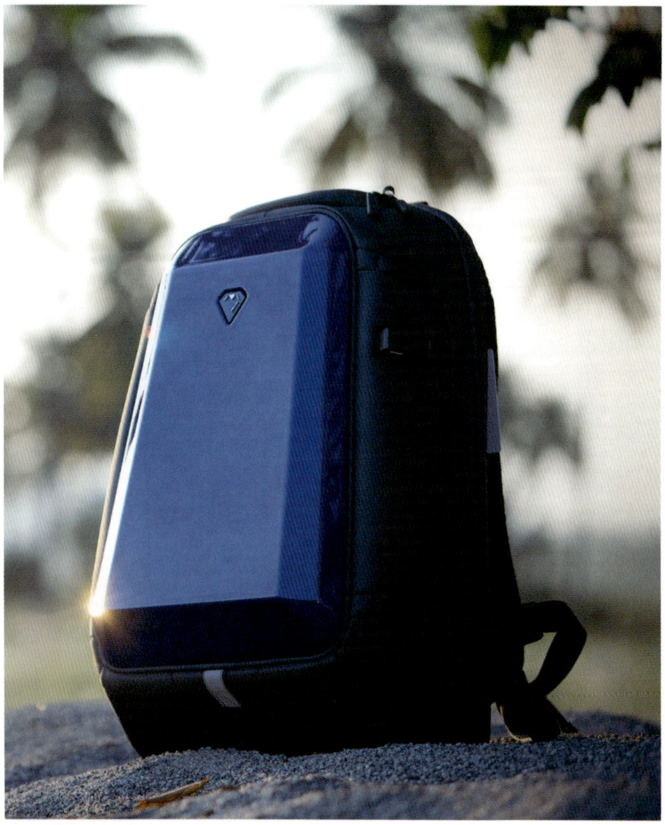

The Problem

The current market needs a backpack that can alleviate strain on the human body.

Addressing this issue with our ergonomically designed backpack was indeed worth the effort taken. Being the first-of-its-kind, we have been able to set up a strong customer base and following.

Assumptions for Design Solutions

- A durable backpack that is impact resistant.
- A clean design for visual appeal.
- Dependable, world class build quality.
- Reliable security.
- All weather resistant construction.
- Smart weight distribution and weight balance.

The Plan

We first looked into weight distribution with a fine toothed comb and designed our backpack keeping that in mind.

Our backpack makes sure that heavier items remain closer to the person's back and not settle at the bottom of the bag while the lighter items sit snugly and away from the back. Keeping the centre of gravity in mind, this form of weight distribution makes something that weighs 5 kilograms feel like it is half that weight.

Merging a hardshell with softer materials for impact resistance is also what makes it a true hybrid tech-backpack.

Discovering

Discovering that a polycarbonate hardshell merged seamlessly with softer materials adds rigidity and sturdiness with impact resistance is our biggest take-away.

We placed the shoulder straps at specific positions on the back of the bag so that the bag would gently hug the wearer rather than hang off their shoulders.

Internally, the dedicated slots for heavy items keep the weight off the back and shoulders of the person wearing the bag.

To go the extra mile, we also gave the bag a seamless flow with regard to the design using weather-resistant materials to construct it and incorporated waterproof zippers.

The Turn

The moment that turned things around was when the hardshell and the softer materials came together!

This helped us dish out a sturdy yet seamless design by incorporating our polycarbonate shell with 600 denier reverse fabric and a ballistic nylon bottom material.

This is how Carbonado earns the title of a hybrid tech pack.

Adding to this are the quick-access pocket for express retrieval of items and a first-of-its-kind industry grade insulation pouch.

Designing

The perfect co-existence of polycarbonate with softer materials proved that durability and comfort now went hand-in-hand.

A quick access pocket seemed the most logical provision to have for hassle-free retrieval on the go.

An industry-grade insulation pouch was added to keep hot things hot and cold things cold for 4 hours.

The shoulder straps were designed and placed ergonomically to help alleviate any sort of strain.
The compartments within, including an RFID blocking pouch, were designed for accurate weight distribution.

Plus, the hardshell acts as a canvas for customization using skins and stickers.

Customization is part and parcel of our design.

Delivery

Using recycled polycarbonate shells on our backpacks helps us put hard plastic to good use since single-use plastic is wreaking havoc on our environment. In some small way, we're doing our best to reduce the mechanical effects of plastic objects on the environment while keeping the physiology and integrity of our environment intact.

Our product is made for our customers all the way from the design stage to putting a price on it. Made in India, Carbonado offers uncompromising quality at affordable prices and is the definitive urban utility gear.

Looking Back

Through Carbonado and Carbonado GT, we've learnt that people are looking for a backpack that provides comfort, alleviates strain and provides reliable protection.

This has already given birth to a few different variations which are currently being worked on that provide the same protection and build quality in varied form factors.

Client Speak

We believe that versatility is key so that our products are used in ways that have never been imagined before. We want to build products that solve problems.

Craftlipi

Making of Traditional Craft to a Trendy Décor by Design

CONTACT INFORMATION

Company Name: M/s CRAFTLIPI

Company Address: Pencil Bhavan, Uttar Maju, PO: Maju, Howrah, West Bengal-711414

Name of Contact Person: Sanbid Golui

Contact Number: +91 98305 99955

Email Address: connect@craftlipi.com

Website URL: https://www.craftlipi.com

The Problem

In the era of mass manufacturing and technologically encapsulated plastic life, we are forgetting the basics of life: living close to nature with natural ambience. We found the opportunity to work on natural material where few elements in décor can create an ambience filled with feelings and emotions. We started with clay: experimented to get life in terracotta – in the forms, functions and emotions.

The Plan

We wished to retain the DNA of the natural material and its relationship with life. We teamed up with people who are having little creative and jugaad mind set and enhanced them with proper design inputs and facility with modern technology.

Discovering

We discovered and are still discovering many interesting facts about clay while we are finding new areas of applications. We are constantly developing new ways to play with that material which is having multiple degrees of constrains and much more complexity and unpredictability than any engineering materials.

The Turn

We spent almost a year on experimentation full of failures to achieve the desired shape by design and quality of finished products. The turning point was in May 2017 when people from an organized retail chain visited our set up and realized the potential in the work we are doing, and we bagged the very first order of bulk supply of terracotta decorative lights.

Designing

We believe in learning every day to deliver better results tomorrow. Experience of Designlipi team is helping the team of Craftlipi to make and deliver modern terracotta products and having a business strategy stitched with design strategy to develop series of products in lighting, décor, gifts, toys and utility products under the registered brand name "EarthenWonder".

Delivery

We are producing the terracotta part of the product in-house with a modern set up along with support of design and engineering from the team of Designlipi. All the other components are locally sourced from small manufacturing units by training them on quality and dimensional standards – creating local employment too.

Looking Back

It has been a tough journey since the beginning, but an enjoyable and memorable one. We know the taste of failures and those are our assets now. Our products are available on various e-commerce portals and retail outlets in India. Please Google. We are in the business of creating unique products to add value in life – those are neither cheap nor costly, but "precious".

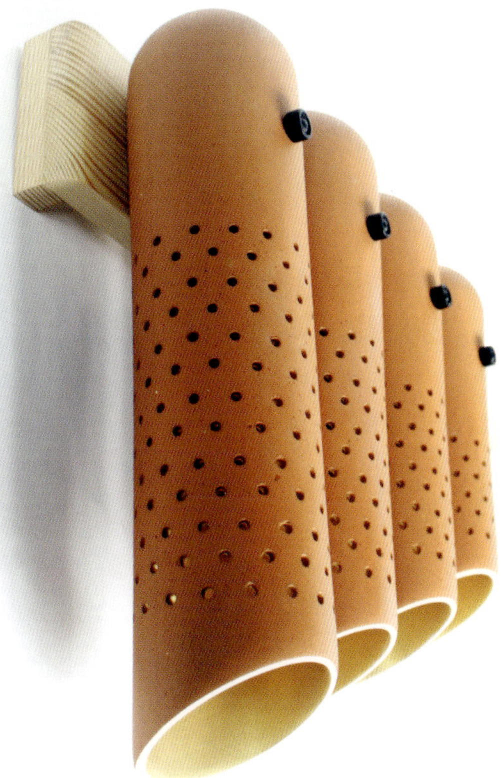

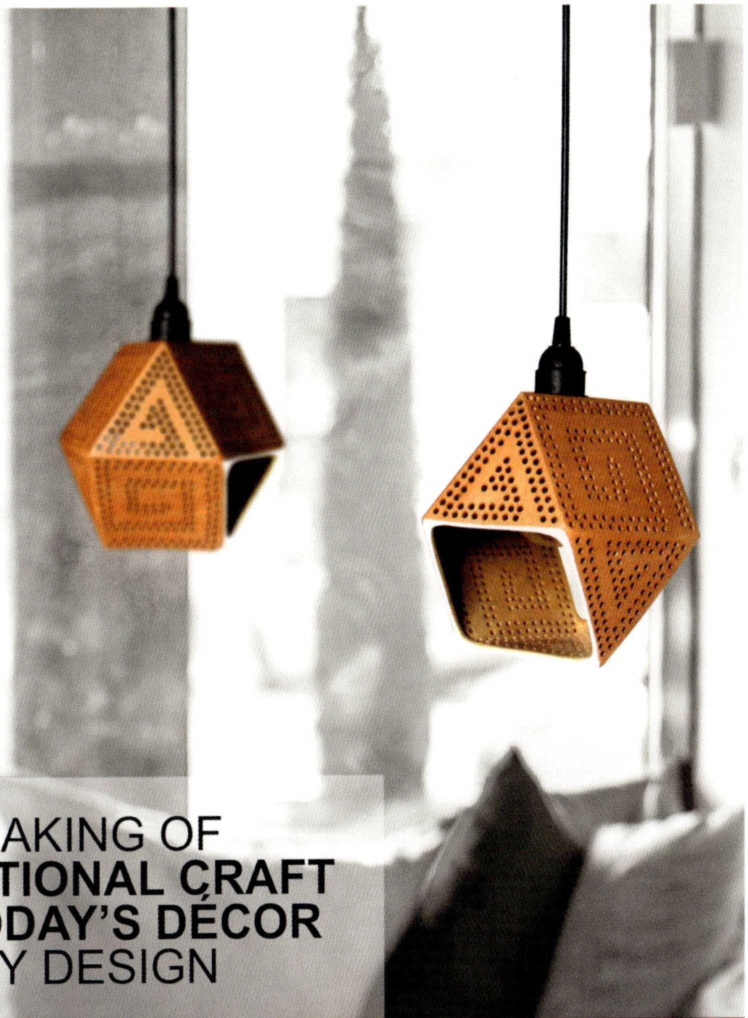

MAKING OF **TRADITIONAL CRAFT** TO **TODAY'S DÉCOR** BY DESIGN

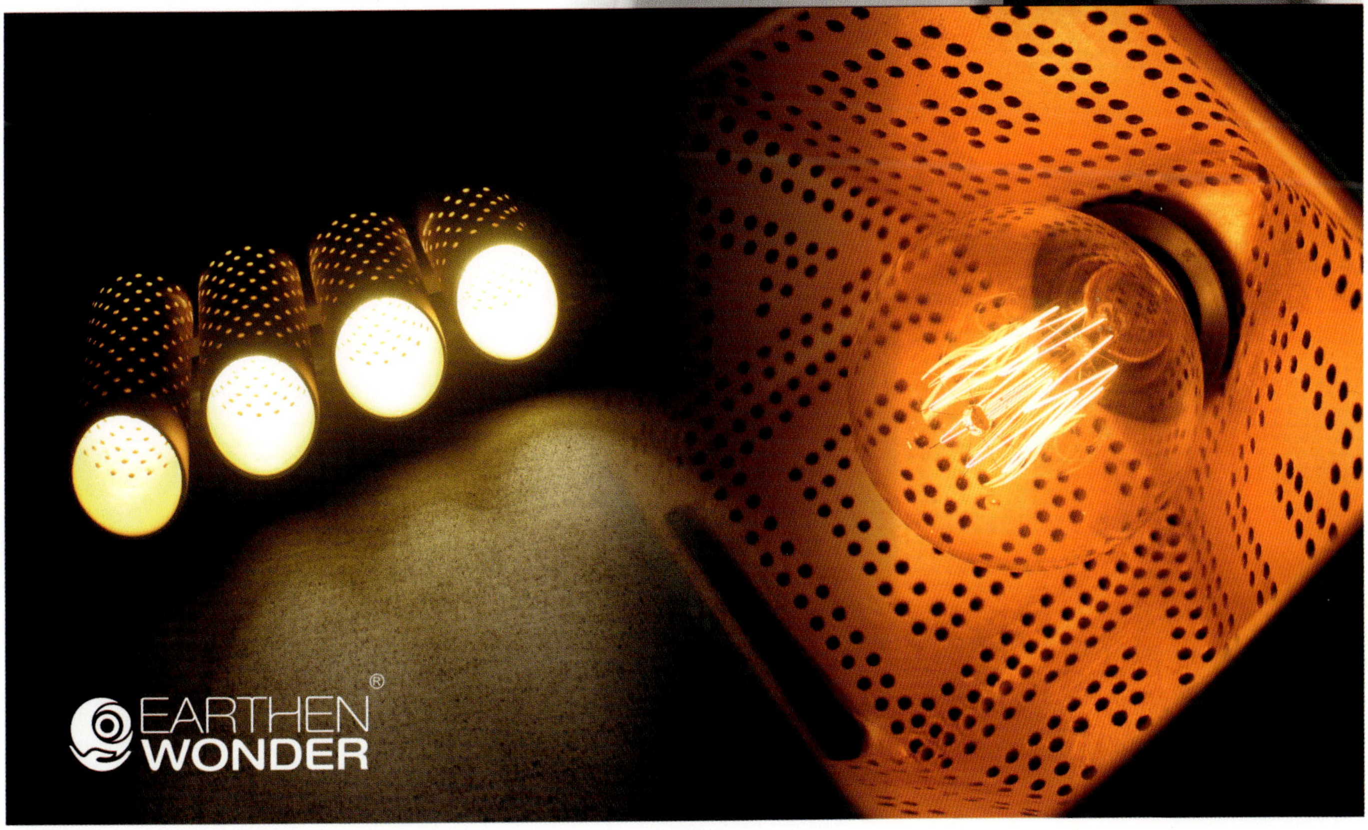

Designlipi Projects Private Limited

The SMART Deodorant Packaging Design: HE DUET, Emami Ltd

CONTACT INFORMATION
Company Name: Designlipi Projects Private Limited
Company Address: Pencil Bhavan, Uttar Maju, PO: Maju, Howrah-711414, West Bengal, India
Name of Contact Person: Sanbid Golui
Contact Number: +91 98305 99955
Email Address: sanbid@designlipi.com
Website URL: www.designlipi.com

Problem

In a highly saturated and competitive deodorant market, there was an urgent need of an innovative and disruptive design solutions. 'HE' Deodorant market segment is known for its macho brand language and flamboyant ads, so the challenge was to get something drastically new and appealing.

Assumptions for Design Solutions

To differentiate – decision was to explore on functionality on top of aesthetics to bring in the pick me up appeal at the first glance.

The Plan

Researching competitions, market segment, target audience, buying preferences and feasibility check on possible solutions to cut down the cost of investment and time to bring an innovative but manufactured packaging structure with available resources faster than anyone.

Discovering

The target segment of users' needs different fragrances for different situations like party, office, gym and so on. Preferences are like strong-smelling fragrance, a long lasting one and sometime for better sex appeal.

The Turn

'Dil Mange More' – it's all about today's generation's aspirations for more and more. It was the starting point to come up with a packaging that could hold multiple deodorants and portable too make it convenient to carry and can be used on the go.

Designing

More than just doing Design at Designlipi – it was coworking with Emami Marketing, R&D, and External Partners. The real challenge began in detailing, engineering & optimization to make it cost effective and to match timeline.

Delivery

It was straight 2 months from sketch book to functional prototype with complete engineering of new parts and was a well-coordinated perfect teamwork.

Looking Back

The ideation, brainstorming, selling the idea, checking multiple prototypes, getting components together successfully in prototypes, convincing manufactures, clearing their doubts, iterating in design, engineering several times and finally getting the product on the shelf is a journey that keeps the tiny team like ours always happy working!

Client Speak

"Design innovation, passion, agility, adoptability and speed comes in mind when we talk about Designlipi. Winning design of Magic Duo could only be possible due to close partnership between Designlipi and Emami team through effective definition of WHY, WHAT and HOW?" – Pradeep Kumar Pandey (Sr Vice President-Packaging Development, Emami Limited)

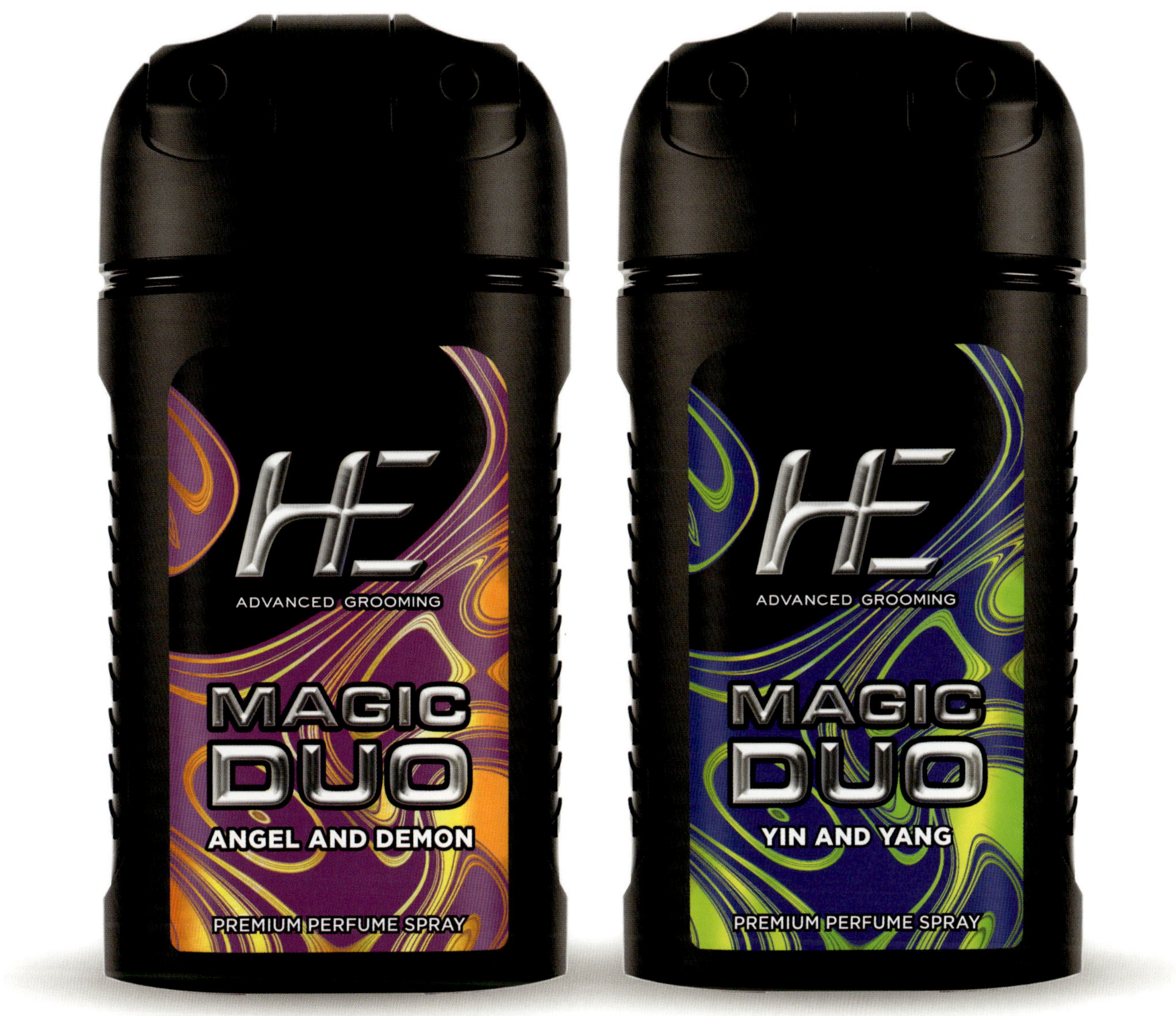

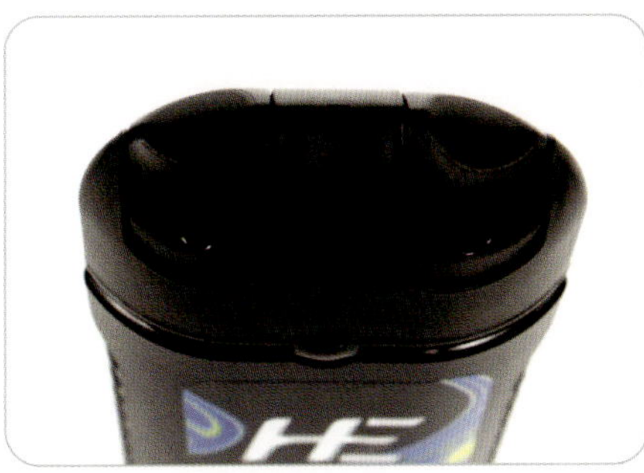

2 in 1

Two Deodorants in
one single container

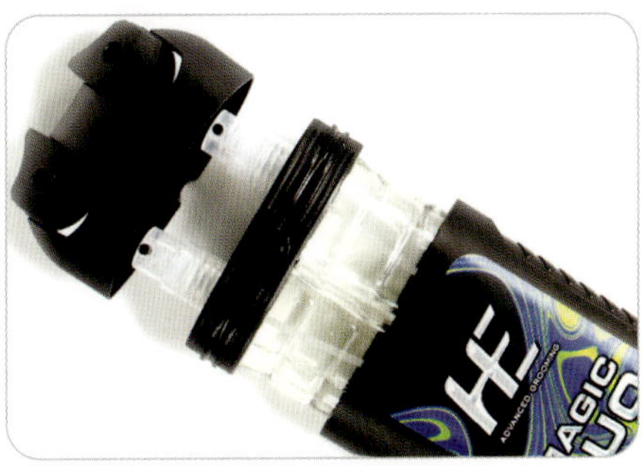

Innovation

Clever design detailing
inside the pack along
with modern design outside

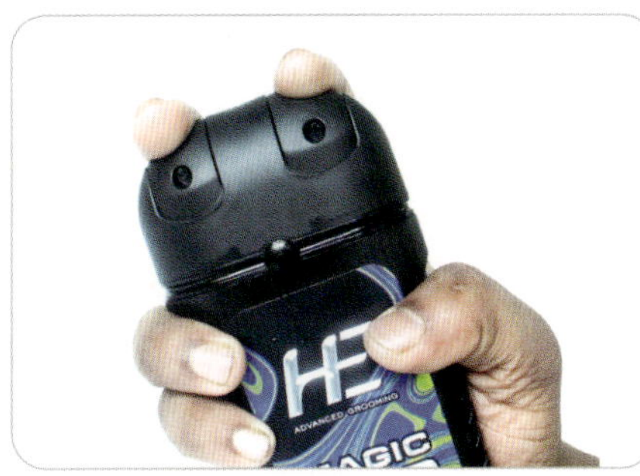

Ergonomics

Designed to be used
with one hand and
two fingers

dorsët
we understand

Construction Key Lock

CONTACT INFORMATION
Company Name: Dorset Industries Pvt Ltd
Company Address: AIHP Horizon. 445, 1st Floor, Udyog Vihar Phase - V, Sector - 19, Gurugram, Haryana-122008.
Name of Contact Person: Sanjeev Munjal
Contact Number: +91 9560999162
Email Address: sanjeev@dorsetindia.com
Website URL: www.dorsetindia.com

The Problem

During construction of an apartment, the key has to be handed to the workers, raising security concern of key duplication or loss and damage of key. Changing the cylinder after construction is not a smart solution so designing a unique addition to the cylinder would help in both safety and business.

Assumptions for Design Solutions

Replacing the cylinder after construction is not economical; rather, an added feature to the cylinder or the key that would not let the lock be accessible, after possession by the owner, even if the key is duplicated, would be a viable way and economical too without compromising security

The Plan

Dorset is a pioneer in its technology and research and development of architectural hardware, locking solution and furniture and kitchen hardware. Such an advancement and strength in this forte of design and development automatically gives the confidence in coming up with an idea of design that will lead to the solution. Probabilities being permuting the pin combination of the cylinder or developing a key that would just require little twitching in the teeth of the key and needs no replacement of the cylinder after construction. This is also under patent protection by Dorset.

Discovering

It was indeed the "Aha!", "Eureka" moment, as the solution was an innovative way of design research. The pin combination of the cylinder is arranged in such a manner that the cylinder is accessibly with two sets of keys and the first set of keys (later termed as the Construction Key) would not work as soon as the second set of key (later termed as the Owner Key) is used which changes the pin combination permanently.

The Turn

The main aspect of a lock is the permutation and combination of the pins arrangement which leads to the bitting of key that can operate through the pin arrangement and in this case if it has to be operable by two different keys, the pin combinations has to be placed in a pattern that combination can be changed only once with the second pair or keys i.e the Owner Key and the first pair of key is invalid thus the outcome being having a pin arrangement where the pin changes its position as soon as the owner key used.

Designing

Construction key lock is almost like any euro-profile cylinder with the difference being the newly designed

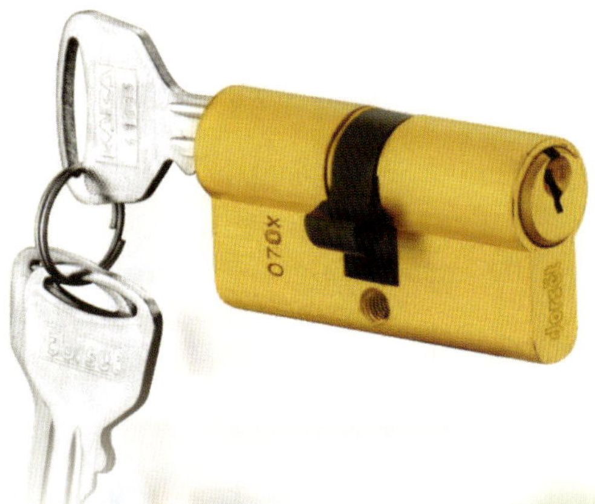

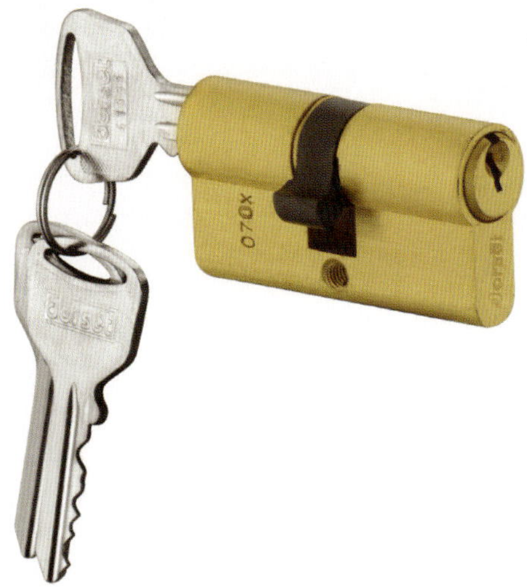

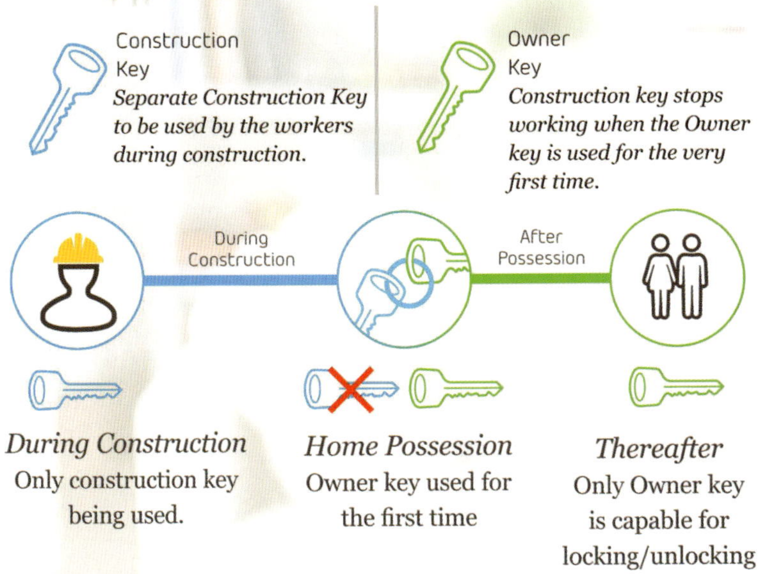

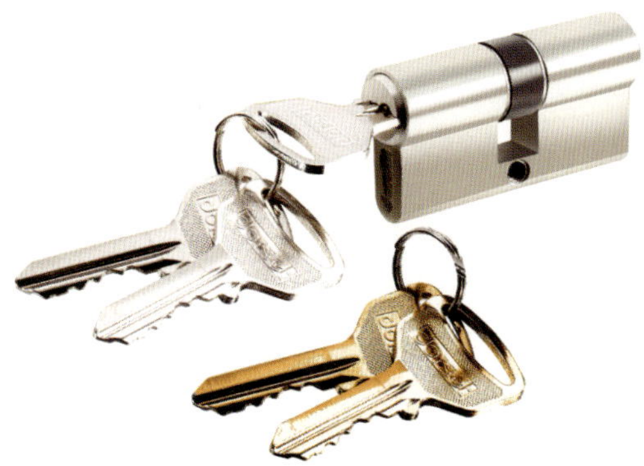

pin combination, so it is equally productive as the normal euro-profile and the manufacturing process includes a system that lets the pin combination change. The cost of product has a fraction of difference than the normal euro-profile which is much lower than replacing the cylinder and turns out to be much consumer biased. The construction keys are not plated, saving cost and time and is also recyclable and can be reused, making the product sustainable in nature.

Delivery

The most satisfying outcome of this project is that the design outcome is a one-of-a-kind system-patented product, satisfying the consumers with secure yet cost-effective living space. Also, being the inventor and the only manufacturer of this product has a great impact on the business prospect too. Innovations such as these are what set Dorset apart from the rest of the hardware-architecture manufacturers in India and internationally, and being a pioneer in this segment, there will be further more development and innovative designs.

Looking Back

"A revolutionary lock, invented after years of hard effort by our team has led to an offering of secure solution yet being economical and sustainable in nature."
—Rajesh Bansal, CMD

Classic+

The World's First In-Wall Water Purifier

CONTACT INFORMATION

Company Name: Future Factory LLP

Client Name: Eureka Forbes Limited

Company Address: B - 601, The Qube, Near Terminal 2, International Airport, Behind Taj Flight Kitchen, Marol, Andheri East, Mumbai-400059.

Name of Contact Person: Geetika Kambli

Contact Number: +91 9821614844

Email Address: geetika@futurefactory.in

Website URL: www.futurefactory.in

The Problem

Aquaguard's Classic was launched in 1995 and became one of the largest selling water purifiers in India. The challenge was to reimagine this iconic design in a contemporary form, while maintaining its legacy and trust.

Assumptions for Design Solutions

In the rechristening of Aquaguard Classic through a contemporary lens, it was necessary to carefully optimize the internal arrangement of components, and therefore this had ramifications not only in design and ergonomics, but also in servicing, engineering, development, and manufacturing.

The Plan

The team began by noting international, contemporary design trends and also the local context and environment of Indian homes. The internal arrangement of components was re-examined for a perfect footprint and internal construct, and its implications on crafting a seamless service experience when installed in homes. Design concepts were crafted to address the best global appliance standards, bringing a globally contemporary, yet unique design language, to an iconic Indian product.

Discovering

While noting international and contemporary design trends, the team also conducted research into the rapidly evolving aesthetics of contemporary Indian homes, to help envision a purifier that blends seamlessly with the local context and environment. Another important area of research was around space efficiency and the clutter of adjoining pipes and wires that impact the kitchen aesthetic. The context of the environment offered both opportunity and constraints into design, and it became possible to reimagine how we might offer a distinctly superior solution while crafting a contemporary refreshing design.

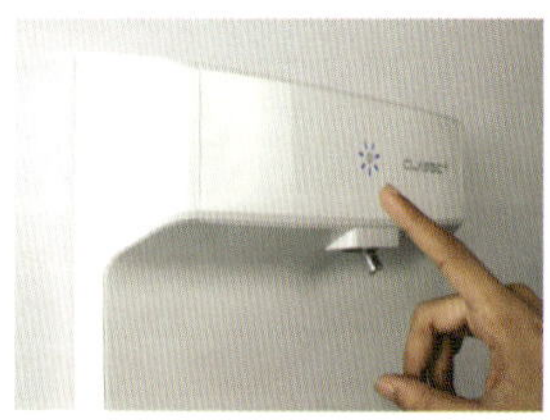

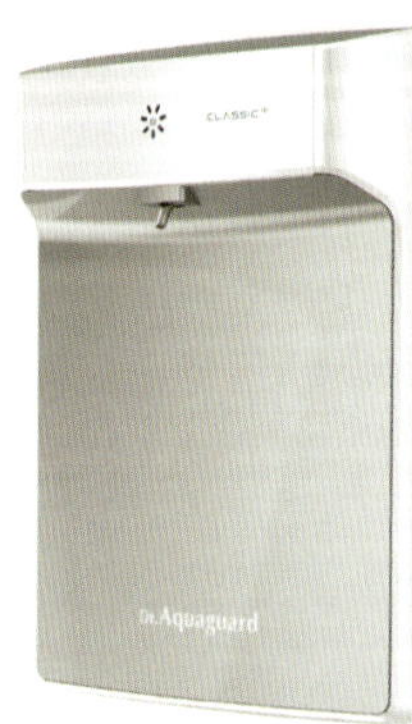

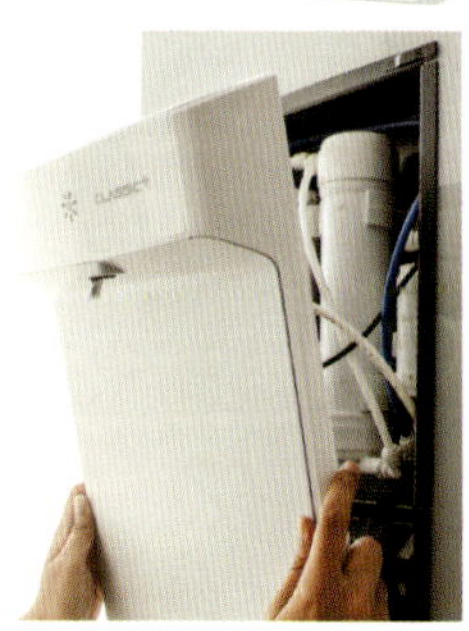

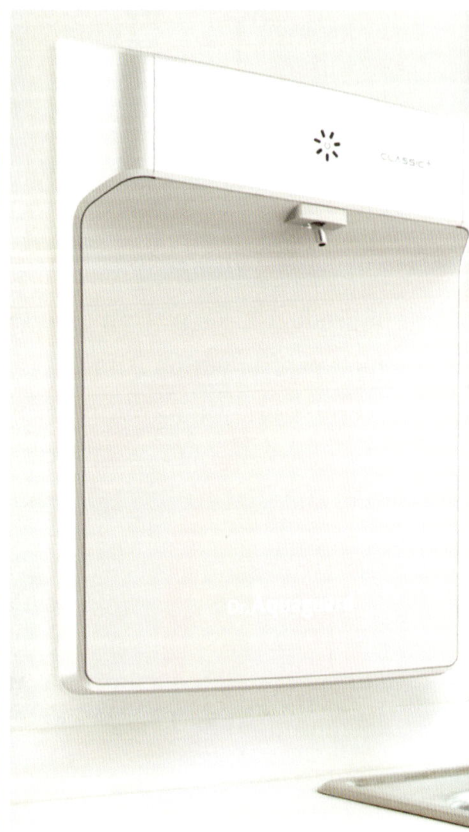

The Turn

The design of Dr. Aquaguard Classic+ seeks to remove the visual clutter associated with existing water purifiers installed in Indian homes, and present instead, a clean aesthetic reflective of a contemporary global design language, while maintaining the trust and legacy of the iconic brand.

Designing

Classic+ blends into Indian walls seamlessly, saving critical space in a typically unplanned Indian kitchen. It reflects the new contemporary global aesthetic and also the aspiration of an upscale living style offered by the best global appliances.

Working alongside Eureka Forbes, the optimized arrangement of internal components enabled the team to create a particularly slim, compact and sleek product. The neutral color palette reinforces its clean and minimal design language. Its chamfered edges form a sort of bevel that creates the right balance between a simple appearance – which is the prerequisite for durability – and greatest possible ease of use.

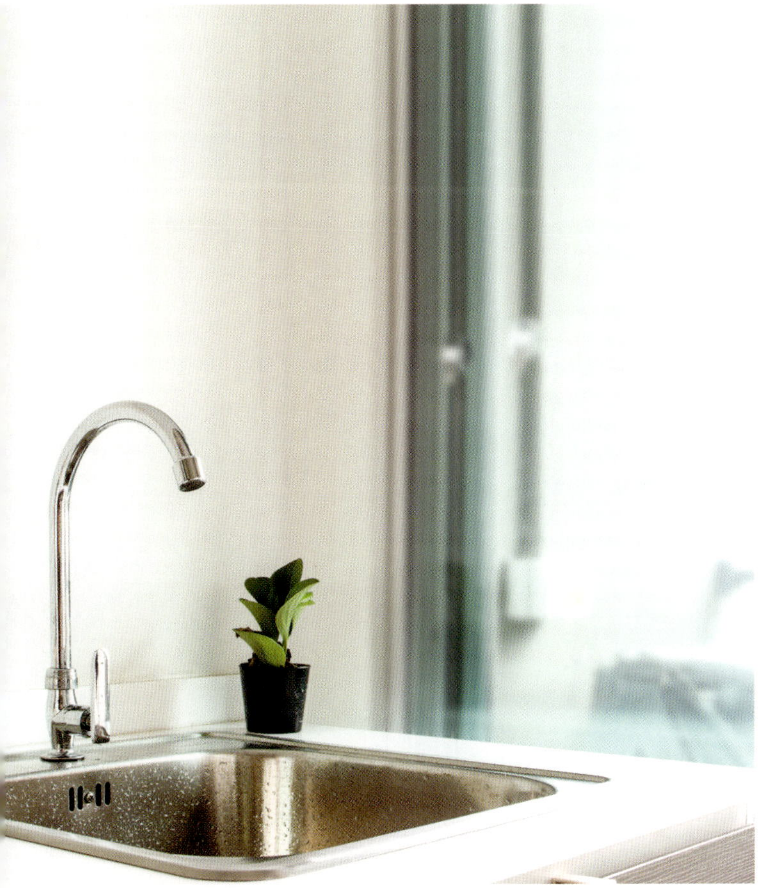

Delivery

Classic+ is made with a unibody plastic, keeping it recycle friendly and discouraging surplus wastage, reflecting the new values of the future around sustainability and environmental consciousness. The minimal design of the front cover ensures the use of minimum plastic parts. The back cover, that goes inside the wall, is made of sheet metal using conventional processes, eliminating the need for any special tooling. Functional components are mounted on the rear casing that goes inside the wall, giving the front panel a flush, sleek and futuristic aesthetic.

The interface of Classic+ is minimal just like its form, featuring a one-point operation. The blinking LED indicator integrated with a CapSense button intuitively signals the activation, the status of operation and the service requirement of the device. The product assembly allows for quick and easy servicing through the removal of its front casing, that is held onto the main body using discreet button magnets. This ensures an effortless, tool-free and ergonomic service.

Looking Back

The launch of Classic+ was unprecedented in the high level of new product acceptance and excitement expressed by all stakeholders including trade, salesforce, and consumers. The design was awarded what is arguably the world's most prestigious design award, the Red Dot Product Design award. It was also awarded the Italian A' Design award and the American IDSA design award.

Client Speak

Dr. Aquaguard Classic+ is a successful case study on how an iconic design language can evolve to stay relevant and contemporary, yet retain its key brand values.

Goldilocks

Reimagining Home Security to Create New Markets

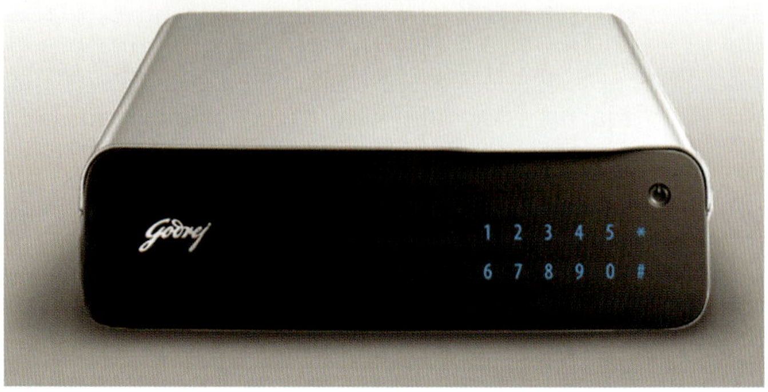

CONTACT INFORMATION

Company Name: Future Factory LLP

Client Name: Godrej Security Solutions

Company Address: B - 601, The Qube, Near Terminal 2, International Airport, Behind Taj Flight Kitchen, Marol, Andheri East, Mumbai - 400059

Name of Contact Person: Geetika Kambli

Contact Number: +91 9821614844

Email Address: geetika@futurefactory.in

Website URL: www.futurefactory.in

The Problem

Godrej Security Solutions were the market leader in their category. However, home safes were still used by less than 2 percent of the market. It was important for design to build relevance to grow the category through remarkable design.

Assumptions for design solutions

In Indian homes, where a domestic help walks in and out of homes several times a day, there is a natural anxiety around the security of valuables at home. Yet, home safes are used in less than 2 percent of Indian homes. It became important to find a new narrative that makes home safes more relevant to users' lives.

The Plan

The approach was to use unique design research methods to uncover the barriers to adoption of home safes in India. Then to use these valuable user insights to create a strategic framework for development of a product platform and roadmap for development. Design would then craft creative concepts and narratives and translate these into compelling products. In keeping with our philosophy of both thinking and doing, the Future Factory team then helped develop and deliver the product by participation right up to the point of production.

Discovering

Future Factory had developed proprietary design research methods rooted in observation, help decode human behavior and explain the motivations and beliefs that were barriers to adoption of such products. One such method was "extreme user deep dives", where researchers immersed themselves in the lives of users at a time when they were most anxious about their home valuables. For example, deep dive immersions were conducted during the festivals of Pongal in Chennai and Karva Chauth in Lucknow, when users brought home their best gold jewellery to wear during pujas. Rapid ethnography helped researchers "live in the moment" and uncover the deep motivations that drove user behavior around the adoption of home-safe products.

The Turn

In Indian homes, visitors and domestic help walk in and out several times a day and there is a natural anxiety around valuables at home. Yet, consumers felt that home safes were not relevant to them. Using proprietary design research tools, the team uncovered an interesting insight explaining that convenience and performance were a contrary sliding scale. The existing format of home safes offered very high levels of security for high-value items (such as large sums of cash or wedding jewelry) and these were screwed into walls and designed to be very inaccessible. Instead, the design strategy was framed to create a contrary "convenient, easy access format, for lower value items such as everyday earrings, watches, even wallets".

Designing

Working with the Godrej team, the design effort was focused around reimagining how such a breakthrough product could be envisaged. Goldilocks, the everyday locker, was designed around an optimal balance between convenience and security for frequently used everyday valuables kept at home.

Goldilocks used electronics such as motion sensors to sound alarms and notify home owners of possible break-ins, delivering "electronic security". While physical security was at a notch lower than traditional home safes, it was a serious upgrade from current behavior of using unlocked drawers. Also, the mobility and portability of using "electronic safety", had serious traction for home use and also found application in several new use case scenarios.

Delivery

The narrative of Goldilocks was designed around the storytelling of "not being a home safe", but a personal locker. The design deliberately lacked the traditional mnemonics of a lock, or a key. Instead, an invisible touch panel lit up only on use, disguising its appearance. The cognitive quality of the product resembled an electronic product such as a router more than a safe, bringing in the mnemonics of "electronic safety". Design enhanced the appeal by an enigmatic champagne metallic finish with a lightly engraved logo, and warm, plush interiors inviting users with well-marked spaces to store items.

Looking Back

Through a breakthrough design, Goldilocks delivered relevance to a market that had shunned traditional home safes. The result was that it not only won industry acclaim, and interest in an otherwise blasé category, but also quickly became the largest selling product in the category of home safes. It has set a new benchmark creating "electronic safety" in the form of a "personal locker" in the category of home security.

Client Speak

Goldilocks is a perfect example of user-driven design to deliver true value to customers. It is an innovation that has disrupted the home safe market to create a bold new narrative and a remarkable innovation.

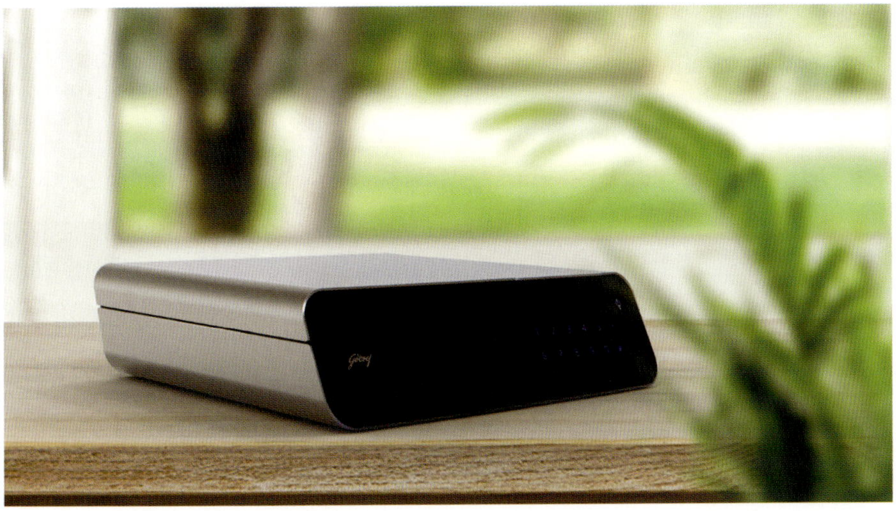

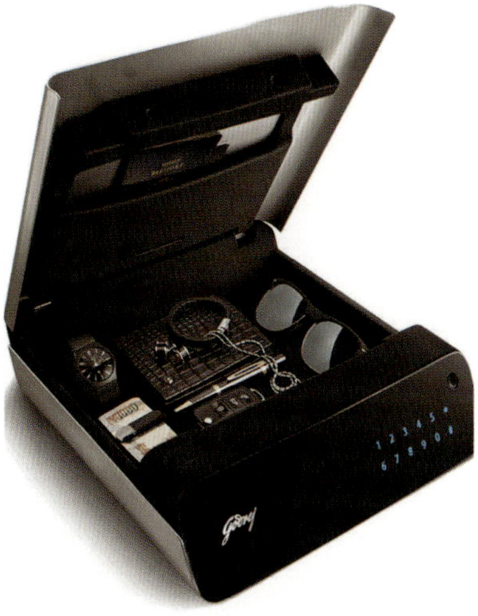

future factory

New York Tiffany

Enhancing a Low-Engagement Category by Design

CONTACT INFORMATION

Company Name: Future Factory LLP

Client Name: Luminous Power Technologies

Company Address: B - 601, The Qube, Near Terminal 2, International Airport, Behind Taj Flight Kitchen, Marol, Andheri East, Mumbai - 400059.

Name of Contact Person: Geetika Kambli

Contact Number: +91 9821614844

Email Address: geetika@futurefactory.in

Website URL: www.futurefactory.in

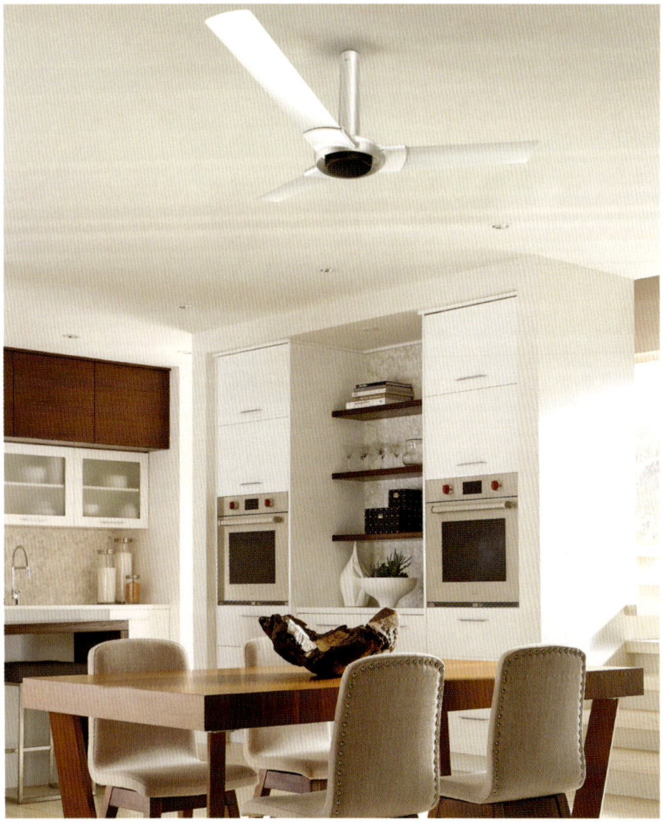

The Problem

The category of ceiling fans has seen little design intervention over the years. Most premium fans in the market feature small trims added to conventional blades and motor housings. The challenge was to create a new aesthetic and user experience with energy-efficient focus while using the standard functioning mechanism.

Assumptions for Design Solutions

It was important for design to deliver a new story around ceiling fans and use this narrative to craft design concepts. Finally, to translate these concepts into compelling product designs that meet important price points and viability factors for a successful launch.

The Plan

The design effort began with a phase where design researchers examined the different points in the user journey related to ceiling fans. This helped mark key insights at the point of purchase and also for the context of use, helping define true user value for this segment. The design strategy was then leveraged by the design teams to create thoughtfully crafted concepts translated into refreshing designs that could be viably developed in the existing ecosystem of suppliers.

Discovering

The team used a combination of proprietary design-research methodologies to identify strong user hooks that would help reimagine the category of ceiling fans. A multitude of research tools were used for discovery and analysis, such as user journeys and personas etc. to create a compelling design strategy. Researchers visited homes and retailers in five Indian cities over two phases of research. In addition, designers and engineers conducted a study of existing manufacturing facilities to understand the constraints and possibilities around supporting ecosystems for a successful launch.

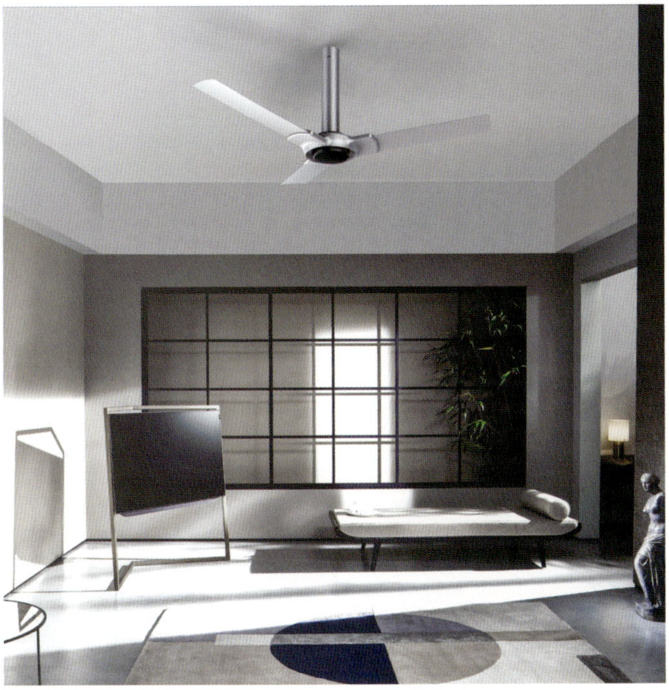

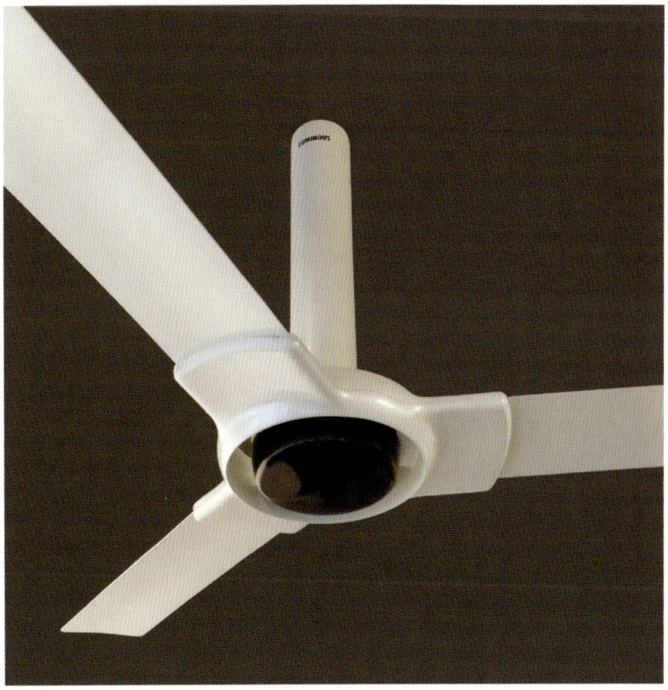

The Turn

During the design-research process, a key insight in the user journey outlined how the purchase decision for ceiling fans was amongst the last in the home-renovation process, and how enhancing this rank would build stronger user engagement for the brand. The result was "Thematise", a product platform rooted in true user value. The recommended strategy crafted aspirational "Themes" that users would design their homes around, with a portfolio of fans to match.

Designing

The design sensibility of the "New York Tiffany" fan is themed around the city of New York, home to some of the finest examples of modern architecture. The design aims to find the right interpretation of this spectacular modern aesthetic to appeal to the expectations of a contemporary Indian market. Tiffany falls under Signature Series: New York. The product was globally acclaimed by the prestigious Italian A' Design award.

Delivery

In India where there is power fluctuation and people are conservative on electricity bills, "Tiffany" comes inbuilt with a BLDC motor helping make the fan energy efficient. This motor features high-efficiency and power-saving advantage relative to other fan motors in sync with Indian customers' needs. The unique canopy-free design gives a seamless look and the design creates an illusions of floating blades. The product comes with a remote control that allows the user to make his preferred setting of speed of the fan to offer a seamless user experience. The integrated decorative trim not only gives a seamless look but also allows for aerodynamic airflow which further increases efficiency as also reduces load on the motor.

Looking Back

New York Tiffany was launched in 2019 and won the prestigious Italian A' Design Award, an exceptional milestone in the low engagement category of ceiling fans.

Client Speak

New York Tiffany is an example of how well-crafted contemporary design can help a brand achieve success.

Qube

Digital Cooling: Disrupting the Refrigerator Market Through Impactful Innovation

CONTACT INFORMATION

Company Name: Future Factory LLP

Client Name: Godrej & Boyce

Company Address: B - 601, The Qube, Near Terminal 2, International Airport, Behind Taj Flight Kitchen, Marol, Andheri East, Mumbai - 400059.

Name of Contact Person: Geetika Kambli

Contact Number: +91 9821614844

Email Address: geetika@futurefactory.in

Website URL: www.futurefactory.in

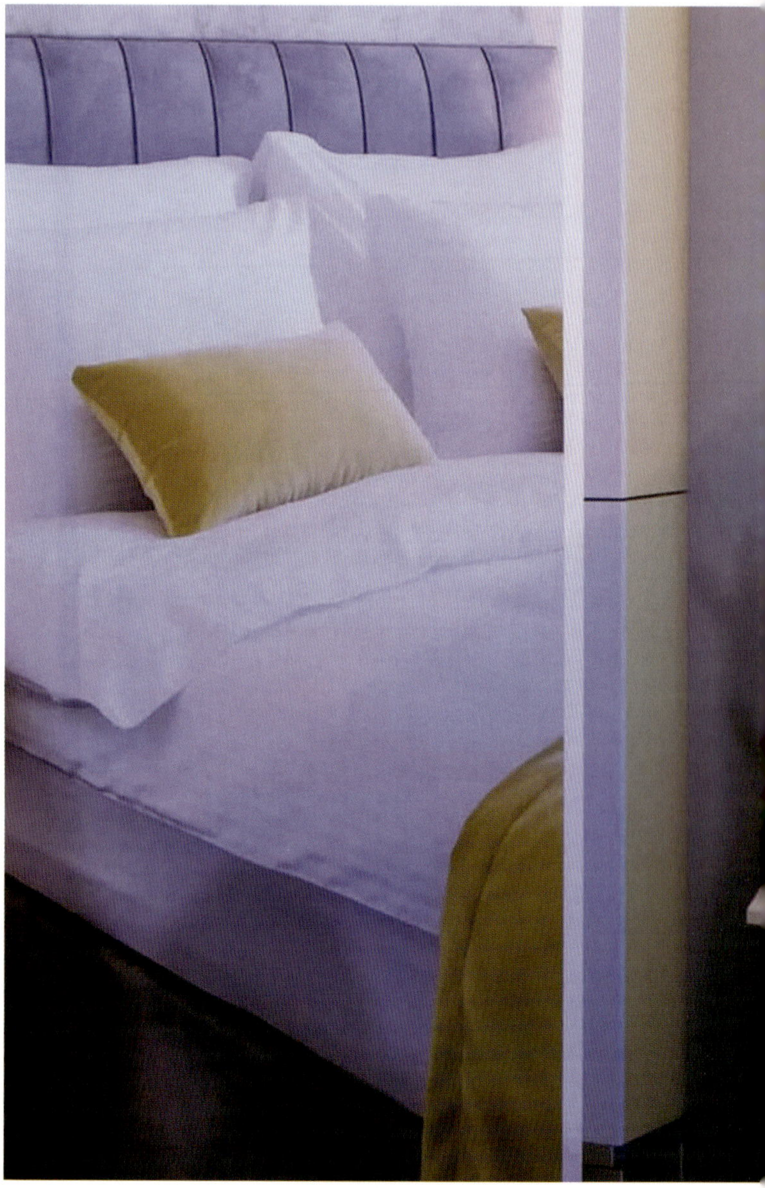

The Problem

As leaders in appliance design, Future Factory and Godrej worked to innovate for a cooling solution that was not only sustainable, but also a remarkably good fit for new user applications.

Assumptions for Design Solutions

Thermoelectric technology provided the opportunity for a sustainable refrigeration solution that was likely to be frost free, noise free, and inverter compatible. It was important for design to leverage this technology to deliver the perfect performance, and craft a cost-effective product that offered a seamless experience.

The Plan

Thermoelectric technology provided the opportunity for an innovative solution, but design had to embed this core technology into a feasible, viable product. One that could find application for a perfect use case around the hospitality segment. There was a significant effort around design and engineering, and around creating proof of concepts and delivering successful innovation by addressing real technological and commercial risks.

Discovering

The main challenge for the Future Factory and Godrej team was in the used of this technology to create a viable format for the retail and hospitality segment in India, as it was important that this design would offer a compelling product for this new segment of users. Through early discovery sessions, the functional

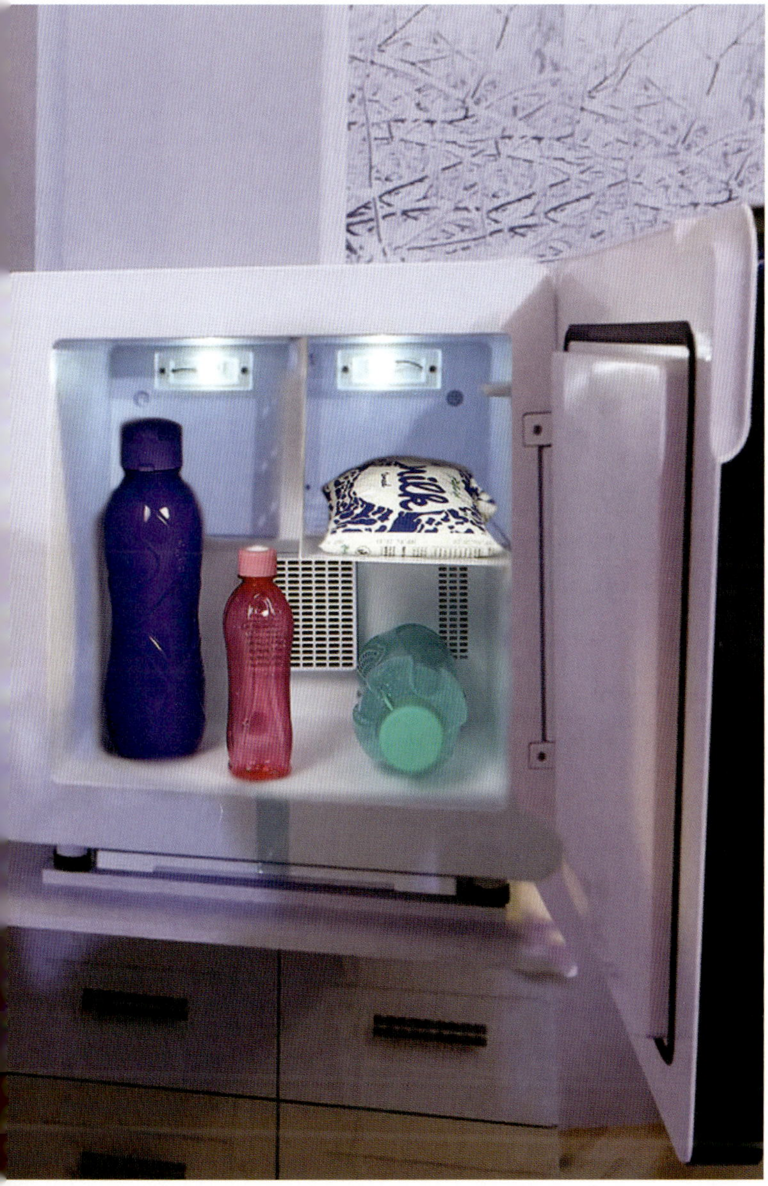

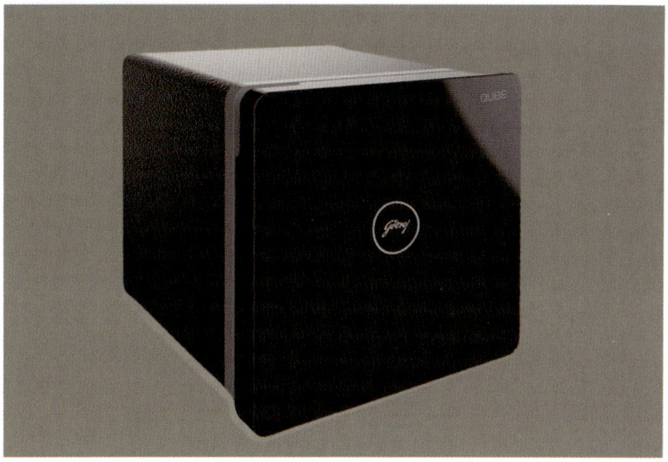

expectations of such a refrigeration solution in the retail and hospitality segment became clear, as did the ergonomic requirements and specific use case scenarios. And this offered a staring premise to create the "right" cooling solution for such users.

The Turn

Functionally, design had to deliver the promise of the right cooling performance for the most demanding use case, and then manifest it in a cost-effective product. An important approach was the use of the thermoelectric technology in a cubical product format, which created an efficient use of space, giving rise to the iconic cubical design of the "QUBE".

Designing

The manifestation of the thermoelectric technology through the cubical design of the "Qube" helped create an iconic product through design, crafting an interesting story around a new disruptive technology. Functionally, the cubical design offers a compact footprint and efficient storage capacity. Moreover, the product has a silent operation which works well for the user experience offered in the hospitality industry. Branded a "personal cooling solution", it is also ideal as a personal device suited for various living and work spaces, taking the refrigerator out of the kitchen, and into bedrooms and hotel rooms.

Delivery

The Qube was launched in 2019, with much interest and admirable success. Early feedback from users were about the delight from the noiseless operation and the no-frost feature from such an unusually small product. The early success also stemmed from its application on a 12V battery, making it uniquely portable and personal.

Looking Back

The new technology brought unprecedented sustainable design to refrigeration, heralding a new benchmark in sustainable refrigeration.

Client Speak

Qube is a demonstration that innovation can deliver unprecedented value for society and users.

Godrej **interio**

Upbeat Workspace

CONTACT INFORMATION

Company Name: Interio Division

Company Address: Plant 13 Annexe 2nd Floor, Godrej & Boyce Mfg. Co. Ltd. Pirojshanagar, Vikhroli, Mumbai-400079, India

Name of Contact Person: Mr. Venkateshwarlu Ega

Contact Number: +91 22-6796 2404

Email Address: even@godrej.com

Website URL: www.godrejinterio.com, www.godrejandboyce.com, www.godrej.com

The Problem

Offices are becoming smaller leading to claustrophobic work environments and mundane-looking work settings. Offices have isolated spaces that restrict free thinking and make the work culture rigid.

Assumptions for Design Solutions

Open layouts are more conducive for collaborative working, but they lack the privacy required for carrying out focused tasks. It is necessary for modern-day offices to be more personalized and home-like which can make an individual feel at ease and in turn improve productivity at work.

The Plan

To create the right tools for a modern office, it was necessary to understand the activities performed by individuals at work. It was equally critical to understand how the same people interact with each other and with their micro-environment.

Designing

Upbeat gets its fresh and futuristic look with the help of meticulously designed die-cast components. These specially designed components were inspired by building blocks that help achieve the desired modularity while maintaining the overall sleekness and simplicity.

To foster autonomy at work, power beam with mobile tables were designed to provide immense possibilities of lay-outing which can replace traditional workstations to create more versatile and user-centric solution.

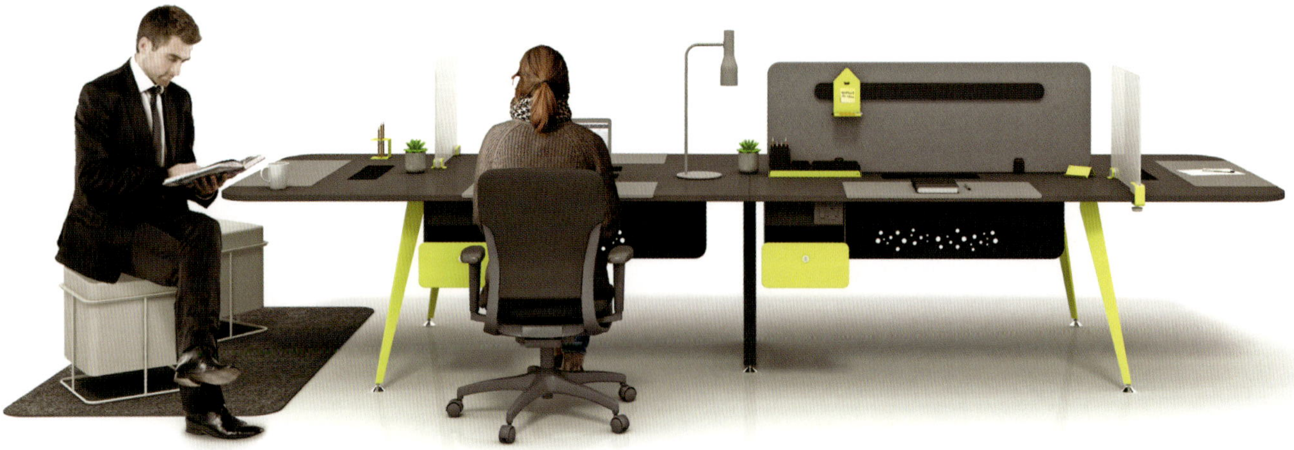

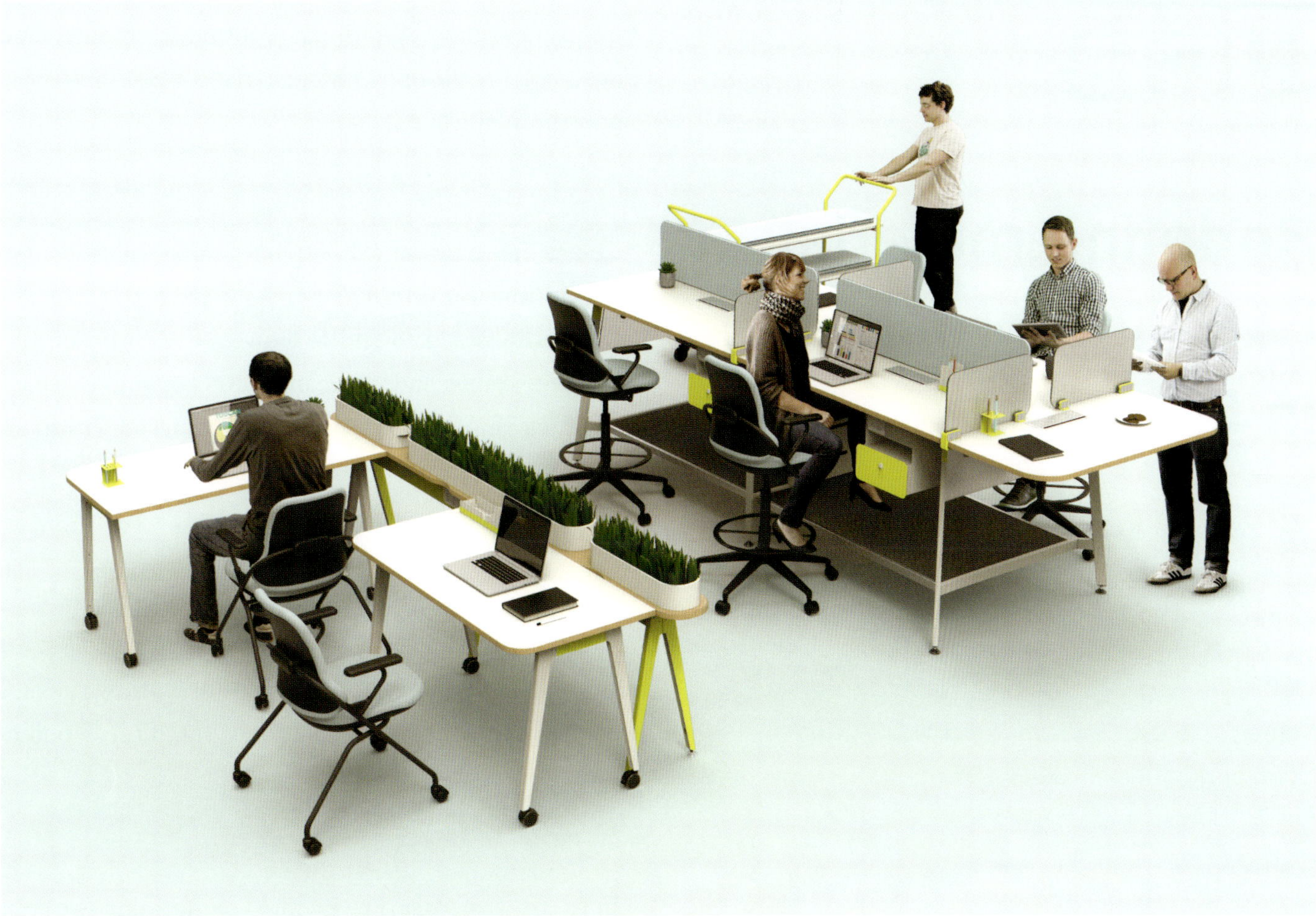

Two key features were added to the system to help offices enhance collaboration while reducing the need for dedicated meeting spaces. Lightweight removable screens at each workstation enabled people to swiftly change from a focused task to a collaborative task. An extended platform at the end of each workstation adds more space to discuss and collaborate.

With wide a wide range of personalization and ergonomic options, viz. personal accessories, removable screens for privacy on demand, autonomous power access with power beam, and high ergonomic workstations, upbeat provides an extraordinary flexible bench platform and comprehensive offering for modern day office requirement.

Client Speak

Upbeat is a new platform with intelligent functionality and a youthful character. It has raised the bar in office design by demonstrating that workspaces can be both inviting and inspiring. –Venkat Ega, Design Head

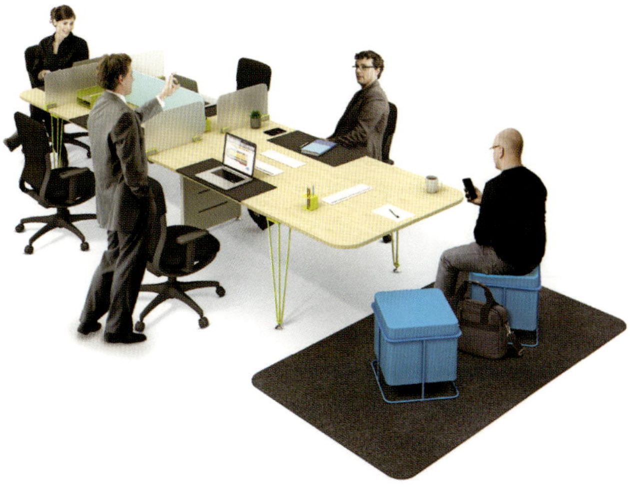

JCB

Redefine material-handling practices in India

CONTACT INFORMATION

Company Name: JCB India Ltd

Company Address: JCB India Ltd, 23/7 Mathura Road, Ballabhgarh, Faridabad, Haryana

Name of Contact Person: Kiran Nair P

Contact Number: +91 9011465069

Email Address: kiran.nair@jcb.com

Website URL: www.jcb.com/en-in

The Problem

In various industries, construction sites and the agricultural sector, there were inefficient work practices through manual labour, which made it an unsafe work environment. The workplaces had to be safer and more efficient, and the space needed to be managed appropriately.

Assumptions for Design Solutions

The product should create the feeling of a safe working environment that is easy to operate, increase productivity and versatility, and be suitable to a variety of applications/working environment.

The Plan

Mechanization of material handling practices has helped various industries to take care of their workforce, improve productivity and optimise their workforce in key business areas. Additional requirement to save time and space for these industries, made a good business opportunity for users.

Discovering

JCB has the legacy of telehandler products globally. We have options for importing various telehandlers from around the world to India. However, we wanted the product to evolve under Indian market conditions, which is low cost and effective to be benchmarked within an Indian working environment.

The Turn

Customers realized the value of unparalleled versatility: unlimited attachments, load, lift, grab and access. An all-purpose machine. The moment of truth was when customers returned to re-order new set of telehandlers for their work sites.

Designing

There are two variants in the Telehandler product portfolio – 7 meter and 11 meter. The 11 meter machine is aimed primarily at construction, which is equally as labour intensive as any other industry visited during the 7 meter programme. In a regular Indian work site, nothing is palletized or banded into packs and the favourite methods of lifting materials above ground level are either using a pick-and-carry crane, a platform hoist or on the head of one of the many women site workers! Our competition is therefore very basic, often very low-cost and we need to develop sales arguments around versatility, safety, efficiency, and productivity.

Delivery

Ultimate performance and productivity – best-in-class lift height and forward reach. JCB driveline – engine, axle and transmission from the BHL, a good combination of product performance and reliability, built upon the economy of scale of BHL components.

The machine application for various applications revolutionize the way work was being performed in various industries. For example, The Casting Industry metal recycling; the work of 4 persons in 8 hours could be finished by 2 persons in 45 minutes. Overall, 10 times improvement in productivity.

On manufacturability, being very high commonality of parts with existing fast-running product, it was very efficient on logistics and taking key manufacturing practices from our global product, brought out the global quality in our manufacturing plant.

One of the key deliverable for this project was the cost lesser or equal to BHL: with high level of commonality, it become highly cost competitive, as compare to equivalent global solutions available in the global market. The result of all of the above was a product that is versatile, efficient and cost-effective, and offers a very high value to the user. In a few applications, customer could save up to 3.5 lacs per annum over their earlier work practices. This enabled them to manage their work, time and space in a better way, while ensuring a safer and healthier work environment for their employees.

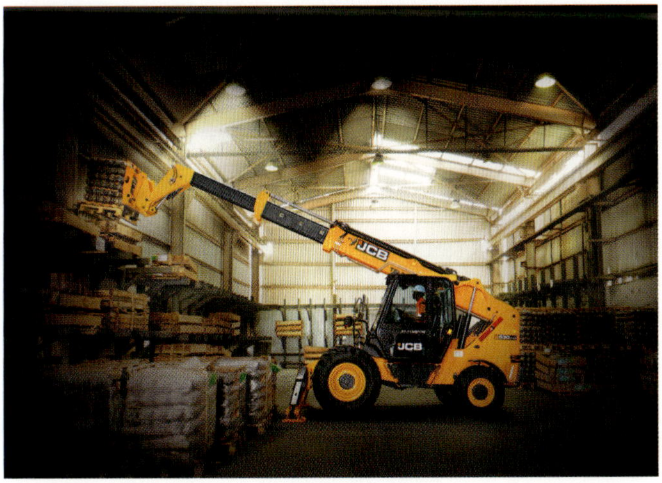

Looking Back

The product was seeded into 32 different applications during the conceptualization and various product attributes were defined while learning something from the different

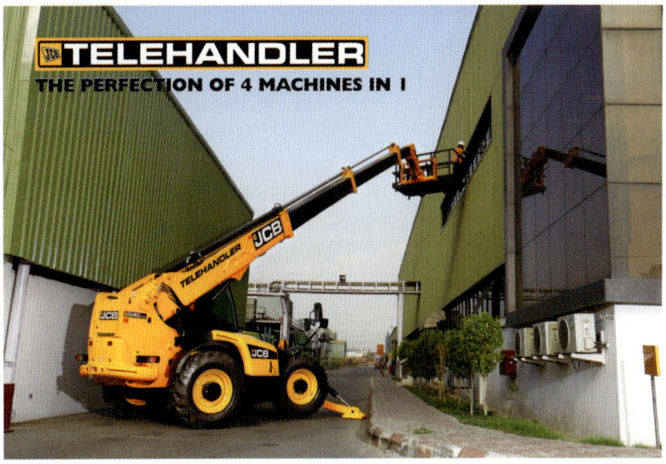

applications. However, the key improvements were identified from two specific industries: agriculture material re-handling and waste re-handling. Specific variants are:

- Agri Handler Variant
- Waste Master Variant

The product features and attachments on both were identified and products were customized to suit the requirements.

Client Speak

I am running a brick business since 1978 as I wanted to be part of manufacturing business. Earlier we used traditional methods to make bricks. Later I got to know about JCB telehandler. It has been a year now and choosing JCB telehandler has been a good option. Telehandler has improved the overall process of brickmaking; the utility is beyond comparison. The shifting of material, like moulded art and soil, is now easy with telehandler.

Telehandler picks up the brick block, puts it in the kiln and moves out the paved brick. Earlier labourers used to put the bricks on their heads, now a telehandler picks up 600 bricks in one trip which saves a lot of time. We are progressing, as the labourers are focused on the core business. Telehandler has amazing features; it loads, lifts, heaps, and shift the material from anywhere. Telehandler can turn in any direction and can easily move 360 degrees within 4 to 5 meters. – Krishnanda Roy (Kolkata)

TITAN

Design Evolution of Titan Edge

The Slimmest Watch in the World

CONTACT INFORMATION

Company Name: Titan Company Ltd.

Company Address: Titan Company Limited `Integrity' #193, Veerasandra, Electronics City P.O., Off Hosur Main Road, Bangalore 560100 Tel +91 80 67046519

Name of Contact Person: Mahendra Chauhan

Contact Number: +91 9880657074

Email Address: mahendra@titan.co.in

Website URL: www.titan.co.in

The Problem

Titan had introduced an iconic product which is world's slimmest quarts watch movement called "Edge" in year 2000 (only 1.1mm thick). The challenge was to create a breakthrough innovation through design in an iconic but otherwise declining category of slim watches.

Assumptions for Design Solutions

The early designs of Edge watches were minimal, elegant and primarily focussed for affluent customers who prefer classical watches. Due to changing dynamics in economy conditions, Indian youth became the key business driver for lifestyle products. Titan Edge has to be re-designed with a whole new approach to attract this new generation of customers without compromising its essence.

The Plan

There were number of challenges in finding out an innovative design solution for a product which is as slim as 1.1mm thin. We began to explored in all the possible dimensions of innovation like form, function,

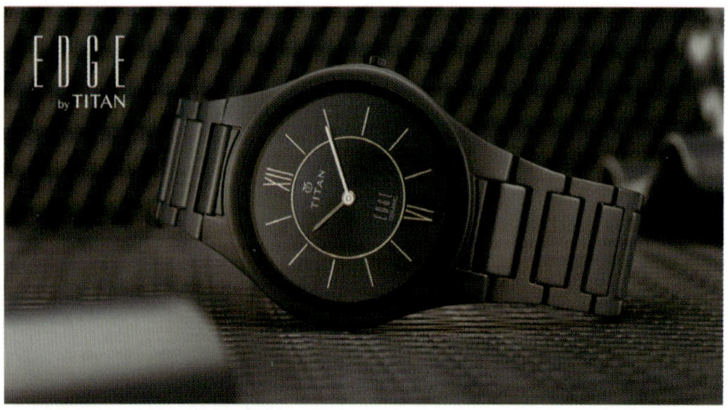

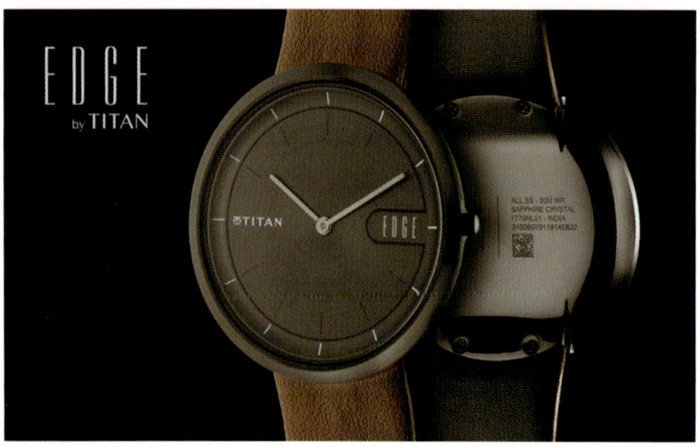

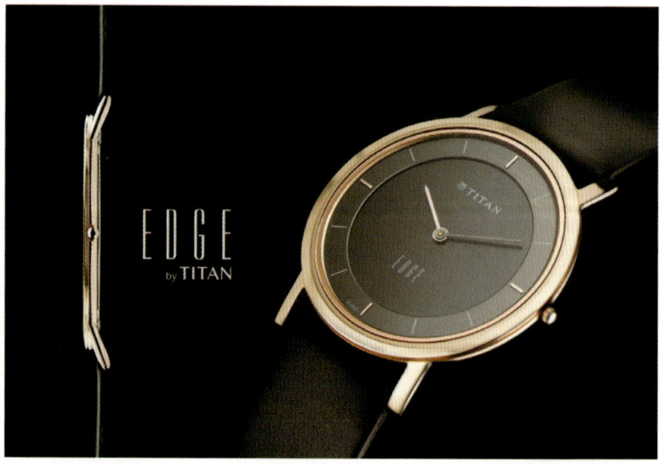

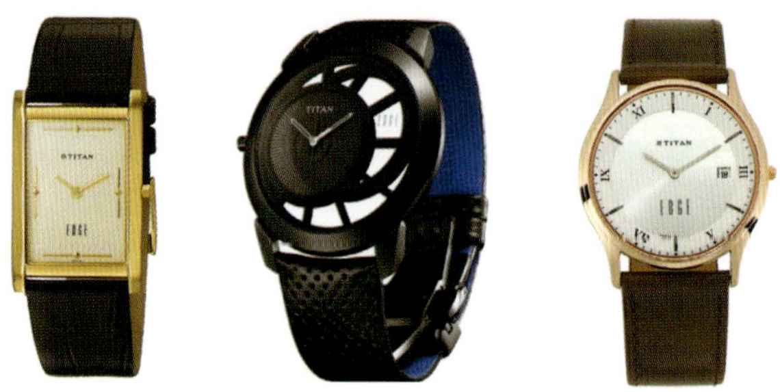

material, finish etc. which could bring the next design breakthrough for this category. We conducted extensive consumer research to find out the changing preferences of modern young consumer. This research revealed that consumers were willing to try innovative products which are differentiated and made them feel exclusive. All conventional approaches were to be ruled out for this project.

Discovering

To begin, we started our research from global watch making trends. We observed that consumers were moving away from simple traditional forms and techniques and moving towards complex features, bold proportions and innovative materials. We moved a step further and took references from across industries and various other product categories to find innovative materials, finishes and forms which could be considered for this process. On the other hand, technical engineers were trying to add functional features which could be added in this movement without losing the slimness of the watch.

The Turn

Our first major success came in year 2010 with the launch of Edge Skeletal collection. These watches were created in titanium and had contemporary styling. They were lightest and also slimmest in the world. The next breakthrough came when Titan R&D team successfully incorporated date feature in world's slimmest movement in 2015. Taking a step further, designers conceptualized another world's slimmest watch in a premium material, ceramic. This year the journey of design evolution has crossed another milestone with launch of Edge Zen, worlds slimmest watch made with sapphire crystal.

Designing

The designers went to the drawing board with a totally new approach and came up with concepts which were not only differentiated in form, proportions and colours but also involved innovative use of materials and functions. In Edge Skeletal watches, dial was sandwiched between two layers of sapphire glass which created a futuristic look. The sub dial minimized the effect of smaller hands in bold 40 mm cases. Edge date was an engineering challenge which the development team could resolve by design integration. Complex micro sized parts were re-engineered into smaller and reduced to fewer numbers in order to achieve the slimness with date feature. Similarly ceramic and sapphire were non-conventional materials but the designers and engineering team created components considering the material property and the quality standards like water resistance and durability in mind.

Looking Back

Every project pushed us to re-invent our thoughts, processes and techniques. The category has grown double digit and average price of product sold to consumers is almost doubled in almost past 8 years. The learning form these categories have been helpful in evolving other watch categories as well. In each project all departments acted closely and supported each other in resolving problems and overcoming challenges as they came.

Key Achievements: Titan Edge Skeletal collection won two prestigious Red Dot Awards in year 2013 and 2015 for its unique design. Titan has filed 6 patents for its slimmest date movement with IP India in year 2015. Edge ceramic is the slimmest ceramic watch at present and sold over 10000 watches. New colours and finish are been introduced in Sep 2019. Titan Zen, slimmest sapphire crystal watch is due for launch and we are hoping for creating bigger success story.

The biggest learning in this journey was to keep trying new possibilities and keep challenging the bounderies. With creative minds and great team work, we can achieve the unimaginable.

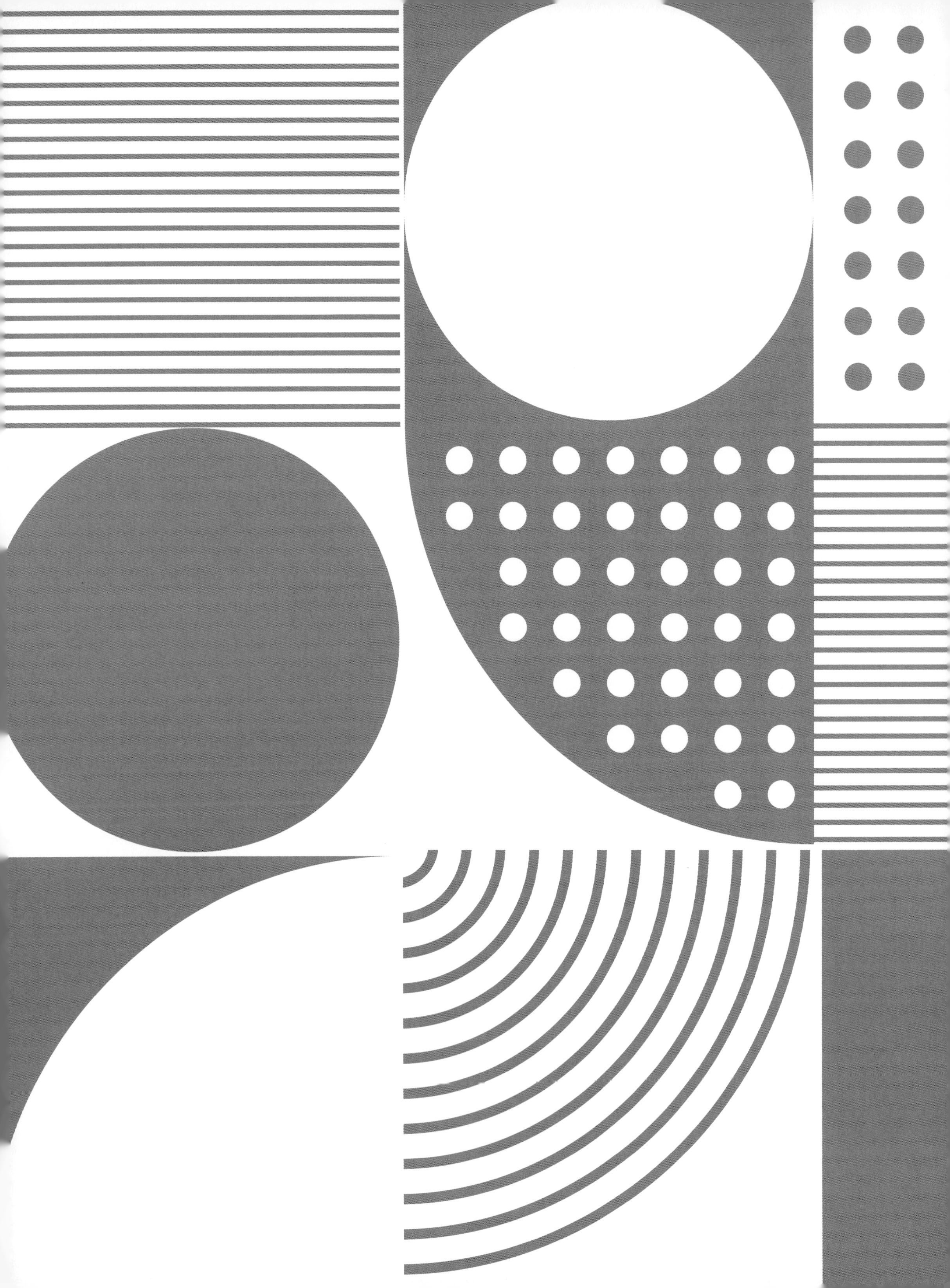

VISUAL COMMUNICATION

Simulation-Driven Design of Farm Gate Grader

CONTACT INFORMATION

Company Name: Altair Engineering Pvt Ltd

Company Address: Prestige Trade Towers, 46 Palace Road, Sampangiram Nagar, Bangalore-560001

Name of Contact Person: Vrinda Puneesh

Contact Number: +91 80 66294500

Email Address: Vrinda.puneesh@altair.com

Website URL: www.altair.com

Problem

Grain production in the villages is done in a manner where the current practices have very poor post-harvest management leading to the mixing up of very high percentage of impurities with the grain. These impurities make the primary processing work more difficult.

Altair went about designing a multipurpose farm gate grader that is efficient, reliable, ergonomic, and affordable, using simulation principles of design.

Assumptions for Design Solutions

Key design objectives to be met:

- Improve ergonomics
- Enhance reliability
- Standardize manufacturing process
- Lower manufacturing, operational and maintenance cost

The Plan, Discovering, and the Turn

Simulation-driven product design in simple terms uses "computer and advanced mathematics, help to recreate the behaviour of real-world phenomenon in virtual world." This approach leads to lower design and development time.

Simulation-driven product design enables visualization, simulation, virtual validation of concepts, without the need for building a prototype. In this project, we have adopted "simulation driven approach for the development of farm gate grader."

One of the key design targets was to use 50 percent data pertaining to Indian women for dimensions and effort estimates.

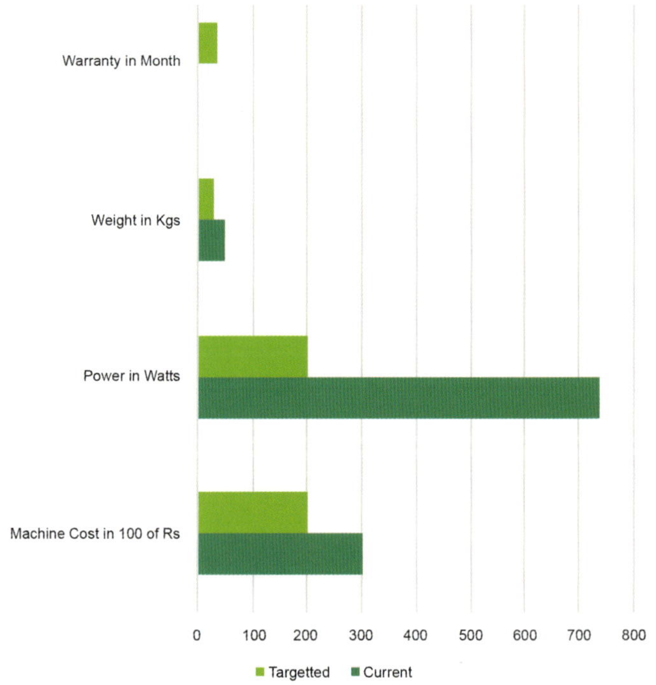

Designing

Design of Experiments (DOE) were done to optimize the grading process as follows:

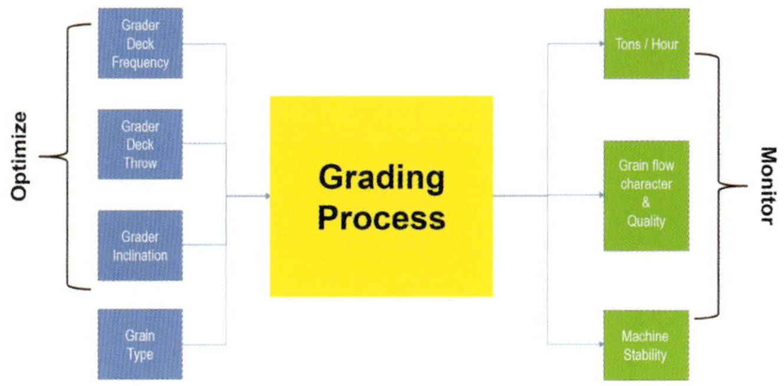

The controllable input parameters were:

- **Grader throw:** Displacement of grader deck
- **Grader deck frequency:** Number of times the deck moves front and a back in a second)
- **Inclination of grader deck:** The angle grader deck makes with respect to floor

The monitored output parameters were:

- Tons/hour
- **Grading characteristics and quality:** Flow characteristic, sieve clogging, sieve penetration
- Machine stability

Data normalization was carried out with following results:

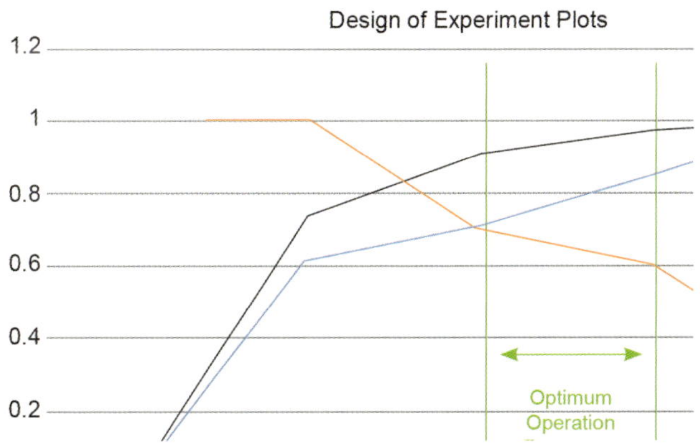

- As the grader operating frequency increases the output, tonnage increases.
- The output quality is a function of frequency up to a 15 Hz. Post 15 Hz, the spillage increases.
- The stability of the grader is inversely proportional to the operating frequency.

Salient data was captured during operation to understand the vibration levels. Parameters of the graders were optimized using DOE. From the DOE runs it's found the optimum setting for the given grader:

- Grader throw (mm) + or – 5 mm
- Grader deck frequency (Hz) 13 Hz
- Grader inclination (degree) 10

The above setting would process an average of 1,100 kg of millet per hour at 80 percent efficiency with quality rating of 4.3 stars. This is the default setting for the grader that was manufactured and deployed in the final phase of the project.

Delivery and Looking Back

The production model incorporating all the changes has been manufactured.

The first grader was handed over to Vennela Rural Development Society (VRDS) and Earth 360 with the following salient technology features:

- Lightweight sieve construction using aluminium and composite rocker arms to reduce the fatigue failures.
- 180 W power consumption making it suitable for solar enablement
- Modular adapter gear box to accommodate mounting of 1 phase AC motor/3 phase AC motor/ DC motor.

Client Speak

The farmers used the grader and cleaned about 400 kg of their grains on a trial basis. Vijay Kumar from VRDS spoke about their efforts to revive the millet crops and mentioned this improved grader will be of great help to farmers to get additional returns for their farm produce, they expressed that if one or two graders are made available for every panchayat.

ANANT NATIONAL UNIVERSITY

Khel

Knowledge, Hope, Experience, and Learning

"Re-thinking Public Schools"

CONTACT INFORMATION

Company Name: Anant National University

Company Address: Bopal-Ghuma-Sanand Road, Ahmedabad, 382115, Gujarat, India

Name of Contact Person: Prof Amit Sheth

Contact Number: 02717718300

Email Address: info@anu.edu.in

Website URL: www.anu.edu.in

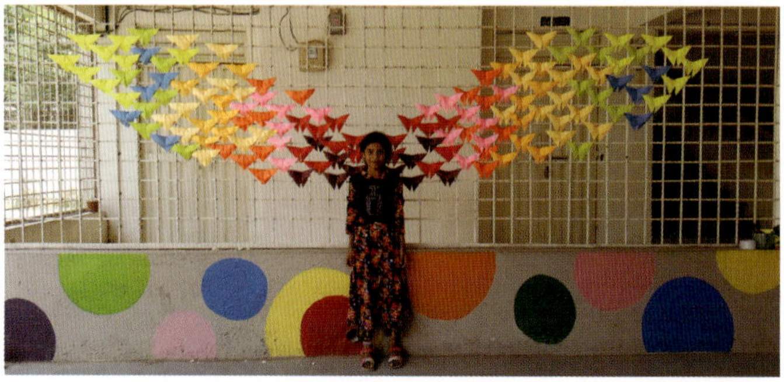

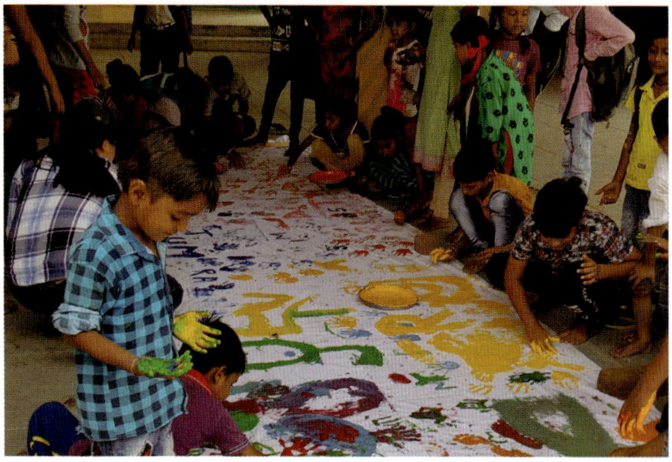

This project was one of the outcomes of Anant Fellowship's year-long action-based learning process, the Live Action Project track. Students responsible for conceiving, developing, and implementing this project are Munawar, Fatemeh, Joyce, Vrinda, and Harish.

The Problem

According to the Annual Status of Education Report (2018), the number and diversity of students attending government schools in India has increased significantly over the past decade. However, the gaps in physical infrastructure and basic amenities within these schools (see National Achievement Survey, 2017) meant that these schools haven't been able to keep pace with the students' increasing needs and overall development.

Assumptions for Design Solutions

Our project is premised on the belief that adding colors, texture, images, art, and design to the currently dull and uninviting spaces of government schools would convert these schools into more engaging environments. This in turn would enhance students' participation and cognitive learning skills. The vibrant surroundings could evoke among the teachers and students a sense of pride, ownership, and responsibility for the school.

The Plan

We began our project with an extended and intensive phase of community engagement in the village, during which we observed and mapped the behavior of students and teachers in the school. After a few interactions with the students and teachers, we began to understand what would evoke their imagination and playfulness. Integrating this understanding with our knowledge of building engagement and ownership through art, we designed and conducted activities such as painting, gardening, mosaic, and origami workshops for the students. Since behavioral change is a gradual process based on continual feedback, we refined and reflected upon our work weekly, depending on how the teachers and students responded to, and interacted with our intervention.

Discovery

Using environmental psychology as a method for this project helped us discover in an empirical manner how student learning might be optimized through their interactions with the built environment. When we asked the students to co-construct a tree of life with their handprints on a wall, with the intent of increasing their sense of belonging and ownership, we found teachers joining in the activity too! In the days following this activity, we saw students and teachers searching out their handprints and proudly showing them to their friends and colleagues. We received similar positive reactions to other initiatives we implemented, such as garden renovation, painting on cloth, and making wall paintings, thereby validating our approach.

The Turn

Our big turnaround moment was the discovery during our data-collection process: we noted that Building as Learning Aid (BaLA) approach – painting images referencing history, math and geography lessons on walls, corridors, and staircases – wasn't helping the children learn. Their apathy towards such interventions became clear when we asked them to read or identify information painted on the walls and staircases. They could not. Learning from this, we decided to infuse play and fun in the school spaces like classrooms, the courtyard and playground, and design them to capture the children's attention as well as increase their engagement with the physical environment.

Designing

Our design process was based on the correlation between environment and the three main outcomes for the children: learning, sense of belonging, and imagination. We used the potential of the built environment to develop inclusive, creative, engaging, and adaptive spaces for the students. We made the common spaces in the school more inviting for students by hanging ornaments on the walls and ceiling. To maximize the available natural light, we painted the spaces with bright color combinations, which we selected based on child-psychology studies. Incorporating hand-eye coordination logic in our design, we conducted interactive workshops like origami and mosaic, and used these to decorate the spaces.

Delivery

Integrating the approach of environmental psychology with the understanding that we had now developed about the sort of suggestive images that did not work, we re-thought specific physical features of the school – the garden, walls, windows, and courtyard. We asked students about what they would like to see on the walls and developed an understanding of the sort of imagery that represented fun and excitement for the kids. We further used this understanding to install origami angel wings, paint a castle with pencils in primary colors and their derivatives, all the while engaging children in these activities with us. Student volunteers from Anant National University and the NGO Prayas will continue our work. Prayas, which funded this project, plans to use our findings and interventions as a prototype for other schools.

Looking Back

Our experience made it apparent to us, and to the school teachers, in a substantive way, something we had intuitively known all along: when children are active stakeholders in co-constructing their surroundings, their sense of ownership increases and they feel motivated to contribute further. The students, who were otherwise associated with rowdy, destructive behavior by their teachers, were now seen carefully watering the garden they had planted along with us, and were protecting the origami installation from wind and vandalism. We saw this shift in perception among teachers translate to improved student-teacher relations. This to us felt like one of our most significant achievements.

ARQUITE

Honda BigWing

Excites the World

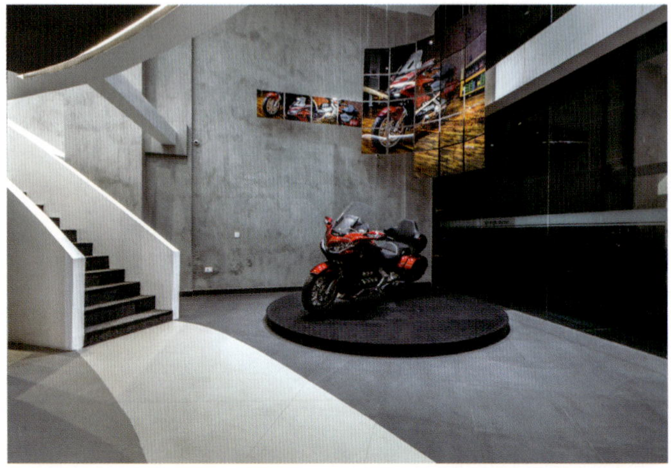

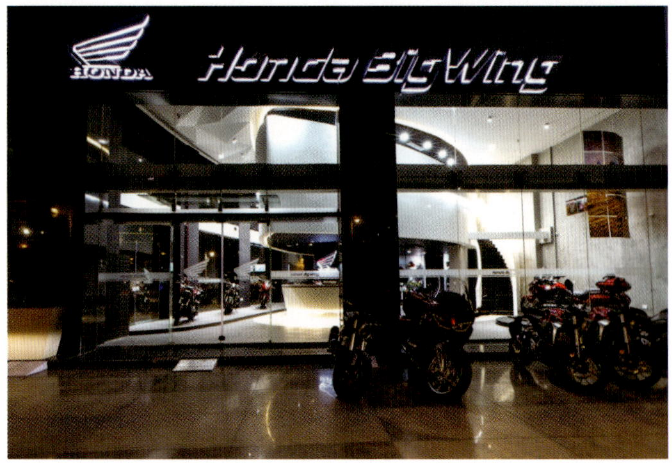

CONTACT INFORMATION

Company Name: Arquite

Company Address: 342, Arquite, Sultanpur, New Delhi.

Name of Contact Person: Mr Kapil Razdan

Contact Number: +91 9310364866

Email Address: Razdan.kapil@gmail.com

Website URL: www.arquite.com

Designing

- The design that expresses an urban and modern style.
- A design that allows adults to enjoy a motorcycle lifestyle and showcase the technology culminating from and backed by glorious race records, where they can enjoy the exhilaration of the ride and the joy of handling.
- A space that will suggest how to enhance their lives and expand their possibilities.

Assumptions

- For our customers to experience the brand through the flow, the following areas will be available:
  - Pride: display area, farkles/accessories area
  - Reliability: maintenance area, backyard
  - Emotion: information, community lounge, event area, test-drive area.
- Product experience all comes down to the fundamental act of seeing and touching the actual product. Make sure that the customers encounter the best products in the best conditions.
- Our customers would like to see and touch the motorcycles in a quality environment.
- We want to display the motorcycles just like they are riding on the road, to stimulate their imagination.
- The farkles/accessories enhance the joy of riding, and amplify new opportunities and the joy of living.

The Plan

Creating a premium showroom for better customer experience and attention by reflecting seven main elements of Honda BigWing experience.

- Fluid
- Futuristic
- Technology

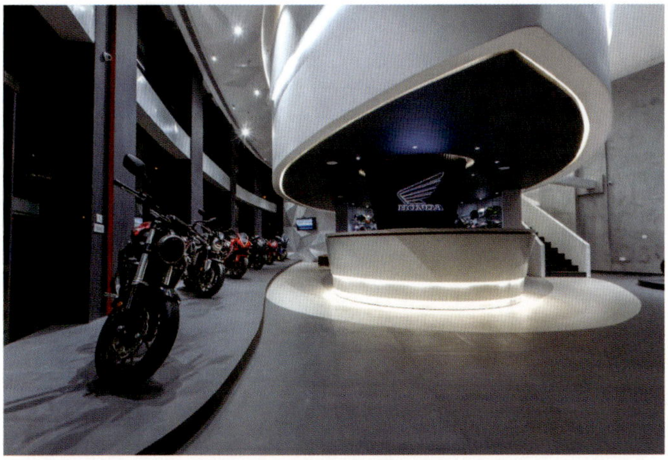

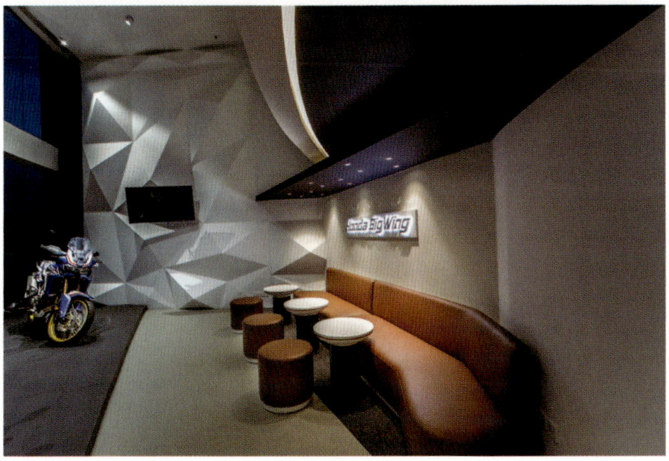

- Distinctive
- Experiential
- Confident
- International

Display of the motorcycles is just like they are riding on the road, to stimulate their imagination.

Material mood board has been restricted to simple and sophisticated palette consisting of glass, asphalt tile and concrete to enhance the appeal of the motorcycles, connect to the outside world and make up an open atmosphere, with colors limited to black, grey, white and Honda Red.

From the very first step through the main entrance, to the moment they leave the gate, we want to create a story path that flows smoothly, to produce a quality experience for our prospects.

Discovering

- Carrying the racing DNA forward, our concept of 'fluidity' stemmed from the idea of 'capturing the motion' and translating it into the visual form.
- The main objective was creating a unity between the product and the place. Creating the relationship between spaces, materials and experiential forms, one leading to another, fusing and folding almost instinctively and creating distinctive futuristic fluid spaces.
- Focus was on evoking emotion and highlighting technology, continuing the legacy, the racing attributes and steering the course for the future super bikes.

Designing

- Located along the main road, a clean/large façade has been taken advantage of, which is used as a display and is easily visible to passing traffic.
- The spatial separation is done for several reasons:
  - To make a more interesting approach for visitors and enhanced vehicle showcase.
  - White clean circulation space increases the length of corridor giving visitors the sense of fluidity.
  - Natural curve of the site is maintained which blends with the interiors.
  - Negative spaces adapted to become interesting discussion areas with a clear view of the display areas.
  - Mezzanine floor was a natural outcome of the fluid design interpreted in both plan and elevation and created an exclusive look.
  - Customer's lounge oriented in such a way that a person standing there gets a full view of bike display on ground floor.

32 Watts

Strategy-Led Design Helps a Brand Hit the Ground Running

CONTACT INFORMATION

Company Name: Cracker and Rush

Company Address: 701, 9th A Main, Indiranagar 1st Stage, Bangalore, 560038

Name of Contact Person: Ruhi Sridhar

Contact Number: +91 9845392848

Email Address: ruhi@crackerandrush.com

Website URL: www.crackerandrush.com

The Problem

Our client was entering a market for dental aligners, which is dominated by an international player who pioneered the category and continues to set the pace in innovation. The challenge was to carve out a space that suits the unique advantages a local brand can stake claim to.

Assumptions for Design Solutions

The category was now mature enough to accept a professionally done world-class Indian alternative to a very international one.

The Plan

The plan was to look for an opportunity in building a relationship directly with the end user without alienating the influencer (orthodontists) through simplicity and charm which would be in sharp contrast to the extremely scientific manner of the pioneer brand.

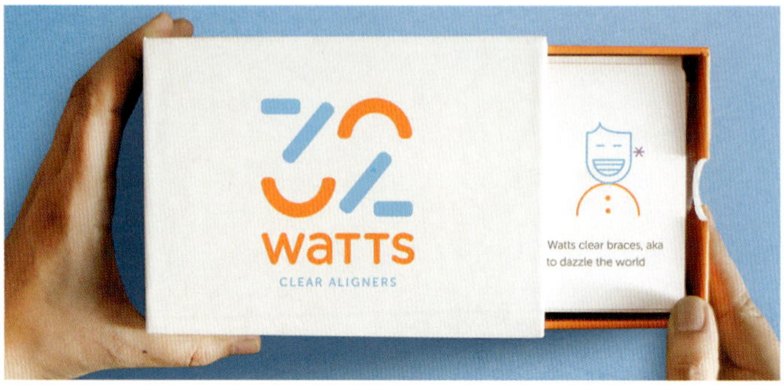

Discovering

While the pioneer had been catering to a wealthier, older segment of consumers through a very expensive solution, we discovered an opportunity in a younger, aspirational profile of users whose life requirements needed presentability and a well-groomed look.

This segment, primarily of women, is now aware of the importance of confidence required in front facing roles such as sales and television anchoring and the smile as an instrument of communicating that confidence. For them braces was an unviable option as it came in the way of a confident smile.

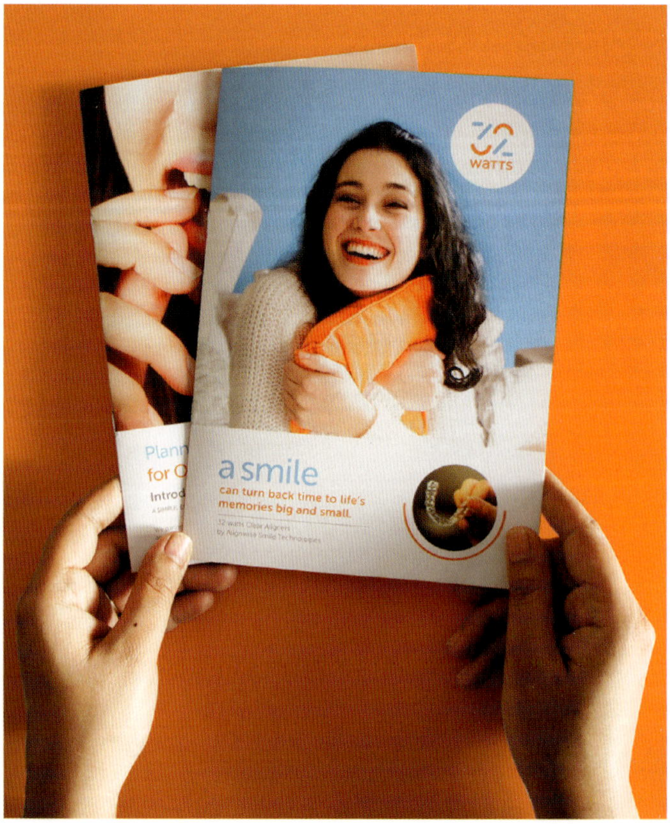

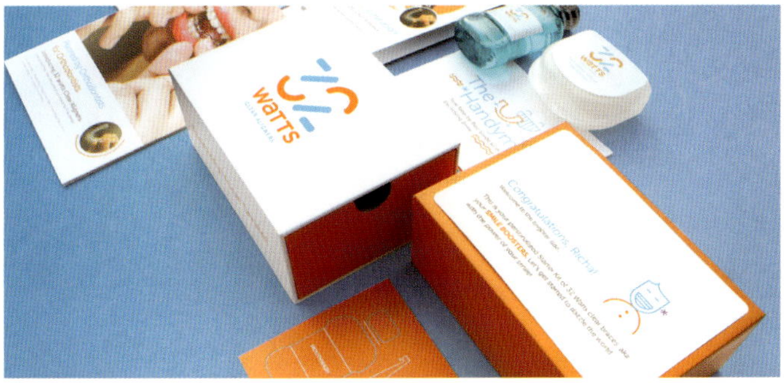

The Turn

The first instinct was to contrast the extremely international, scientific look of the pioneer with something that is Indian and warm. However, we found the most powerful opportunity in celebrating the candid, spontaneous smile as a sharp counterpoint to the staged and engineered look of the multinational brand. This "spontaneous smile" became the inspiration for all design and communication.

Designing

The process started with a name that was more like a consumer brand rather than a medical brand, and in 32 Watts, we found exactly that. The logo designed as an ambigram gave it a charming twist when people discovered how the logo works both ways.

We took the idea further by designing a starter kit with charming little touches that made the unboxing an extremely welcoming experience to the category.

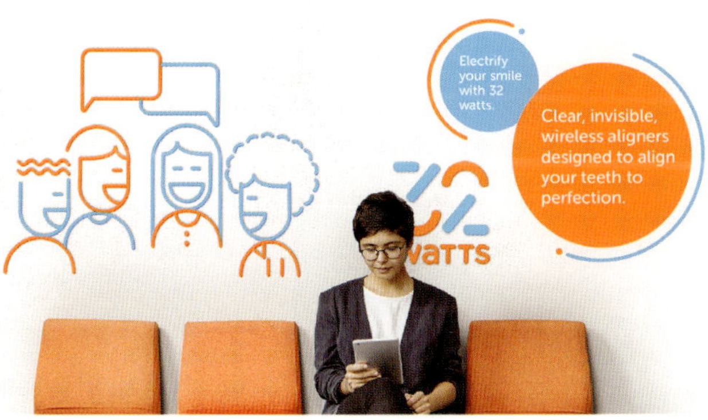

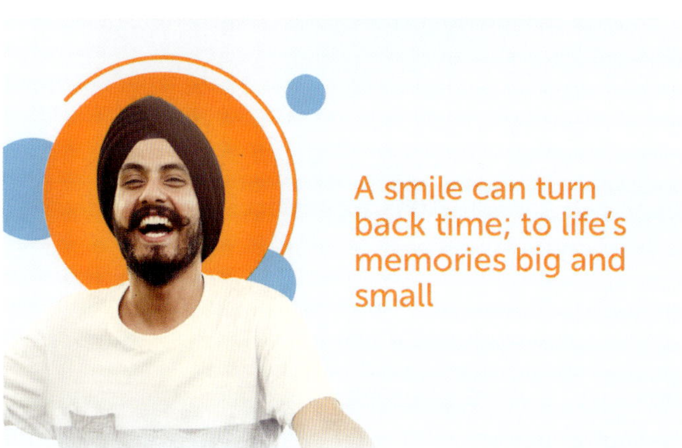

Looking Back

While the logo and visual language have been highly appreciated, the feedback is that photos of the actual product and adaptation into gifs should have been featured more extensively. Since the concept of aligners is still nascent in India, this would help end users understand, distinguish from other dental procedures and accept the product better.

Client Speak

We hired C&R at an early stage of the business launch where everything, including the name, was up for grabs. Both Ashutosh and Ruhi helped align the ethos of the promoters, vision, mission of company with strategic brand positioning. By providing an inspiring narrative for the brand which included the name, 32 Watts, the magnetic essence and all the foundational elements that brought our vision alive. The following aspects make working with C&R special:

- Market research-backed process and the depth with which the team understood the business before getting into brand development work.
- Matching the positioning with the ethos of the company and aligning it with business strategy
- Bringing the brand alive through an excellent visual identity that will ensure long-term brand recall. —Rahul Agrawal, Promoter

INTERICS®
The Science of Creating Designs That Work

Integrated Branding – Nichrome India

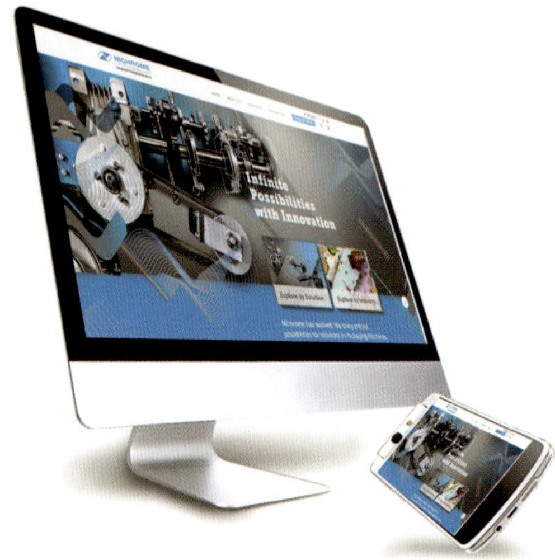

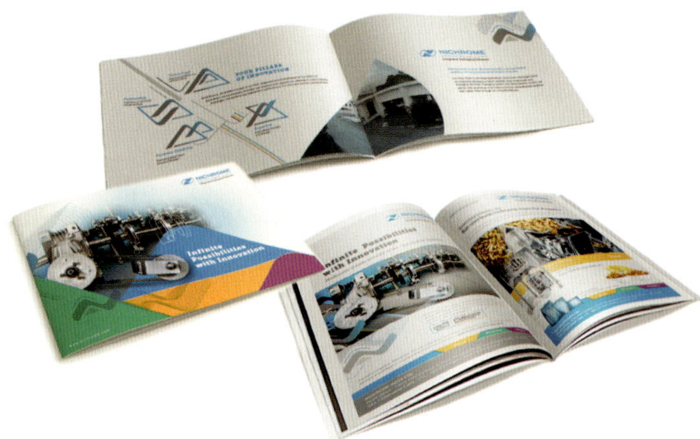

CONTACT INFORMATION

Company Name: Interics Designs Pvt Ltd

Company Address: 408/409, Lunkad Sky station, 4th Floor, Datta Mandir Chowk, Near HDFC Bank, Viman Nagar, Pune 411014

Name of Contact Person: Ms. Priya Philip

Contact Number: +91 9975560588

Email Address: priya@intericsdesigns.com

Website URL: www.intericdesigns.com

The Problem

Nichrome, known for its packaging machines across diverse industries, has begun taking its business to the next level with wider offerings and planned entry into new markets.

The challenge: uplift Brand Nichrome as a systems supplier of end-to-end packaging solutions; showcase the various business units and application expertise areas.

Assumptions for Design Solutions and the Plan

We implemented a full-scale qualitative research to gather data. This helped us gain insights into what both the customers and people in the Nichrome team felt about the brand's current status, and new direction.

To project the next level of Nichrome, the **Brand's DNA of innovation was identified as the springboard** for bringing about the desirable image change as well as driving the necessary culture and strong orientation toward customer needs, which would be essential contributors for growth. We leveraged this strength to curate the brand assets which would signify 'Nichrome Next'.

Discovering

Based on insights gained by our research, we collaborated with Nichrome to develop different aspects of their brand, namely: their core, their architecture and articulation. Nichrome's core lay with the increased ambit of their offerings – and their ability to be an innovative, forward thinking provider of those offerings.

Based on the platform- 'Innovation to Create Value for Customer', a new brand architecture was defined, with three SBUs to illustrate Nichrome's capability of 'Integrated Packaging Solutions': Packaging Machines, Packaging

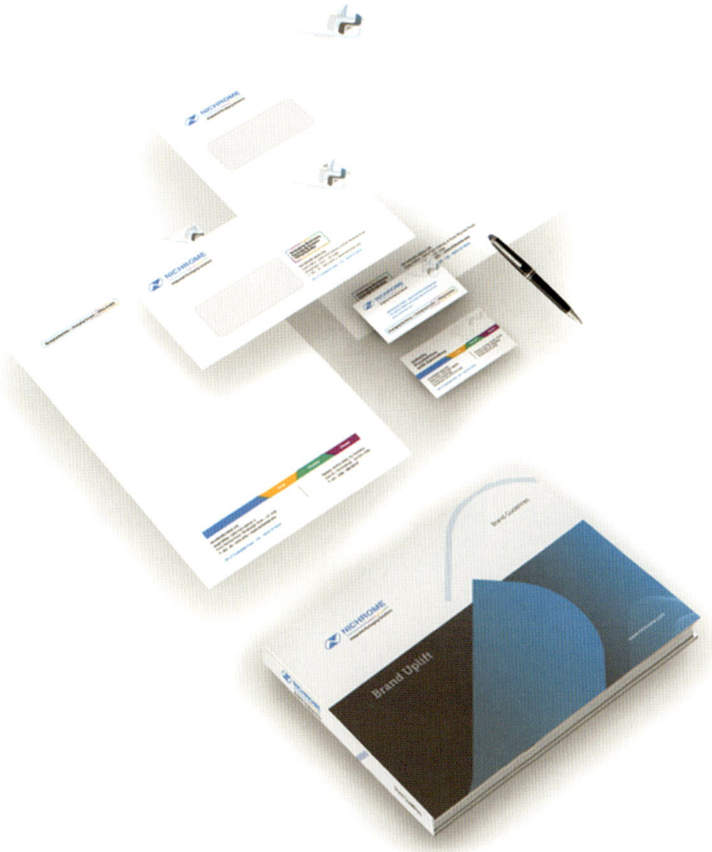

Systems and Filling Systems. To demonstrate a spectrum of expertise, the industry applications were categorized under three domains: Food, Pharma and Others.

The Turn

Arriving at our unique Brand Positioning provided the 'Aha!' moment. We crafted a Communication theme to express Nichrome's purpose, unique persona and differentiated offering through unified Imagery and Messaging.

"Infinite Possibilities with Innovation" expressed the expansion of solution capabilities; unlocking innovation by defying boundaries to create infinite possibilities of value for customers.

The slogan had deeper resonance as it built on innovation which is in their DNA. After all, they had innovated India's first milk pouch packaging machine four decades ago!

Designing

We created a cohesive brand identity system based on different aspects of the thematic brand narrative and to depict Nichrome's innovation process – the cornerstone for 'Infinite Possibilities' of creating value.

We also evolved a heritage brand property 'Nichromian' to its modern avatar 'Nx-gen Nichromian' as part of the Identity System.

The Brand Engagement involved developing Clear and Consistent Business Communication. We developed Communication templates to showcase the brand assets conveying 'Nichrome Next' in a consistent manner, with relevant translation articulating benefits and messaging at Corporate, Business and Solution levels.

Looking Back

The brand was launched with confident positioning as a thought leader, motivating partner, and valuable innovator to strengthen the value perception of an integrated packaging solutions provider; enabling the business lead by the power of its brand, while taking a focused approach to enhance expertise in business segments and industry applications.

Client Speak

"Integrated Branding solution by Interics helped our brand strategy to gain a unique positioning in the packaging industry domain." – Mrunal Joshi, CEO, Nichrome India

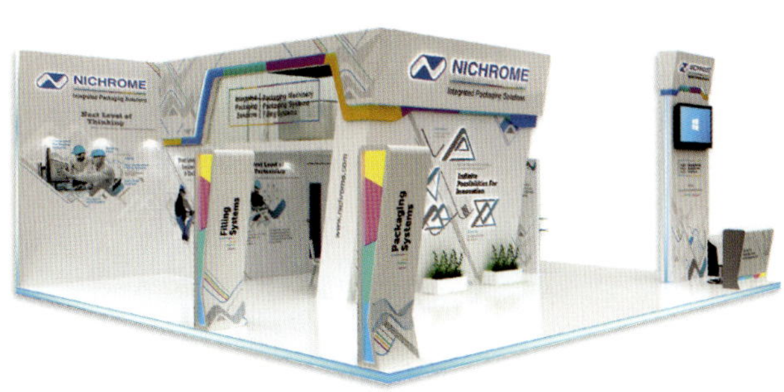

Rusher's Flip Flop Kiosk Design

CONTACT INFORMATION

Company Name: KREO Design and Innovation

Company Address: #3490, 14th Main, 2nd Cross, Indiranagar, Bangalore

Name of Contact Person: Darshita Thaker

Contact Number: +91 9845202295

Email Address: darshita@kreo.in

Website URL: www.kreo.in

The Problem

Rusher's Flip Flop was competing for customers' attention in a crowded and competitive mall space in Hyderabad. The product being something that shoppers do not actively seek out, Rusher's needed to nudge audiences toward making on-the-spot purchases at its kiosk. This goal needed to be achieved through impactful communication.

Assumptions for Design Solutions

It was mutually agreed that, while designing the kiosk, we would stay true to Rusher's own brand colours which were bright and cheery. We believed Rusher's had a fun, young, quirky brand persona, and that would really have to come through our design approach.

The Plan

We decided that a thematic approach would work best given the kind of high-density space the kiosk would be situated in. We adopted the concept of a "Holiday Life" and we strategically incorporated visual elements

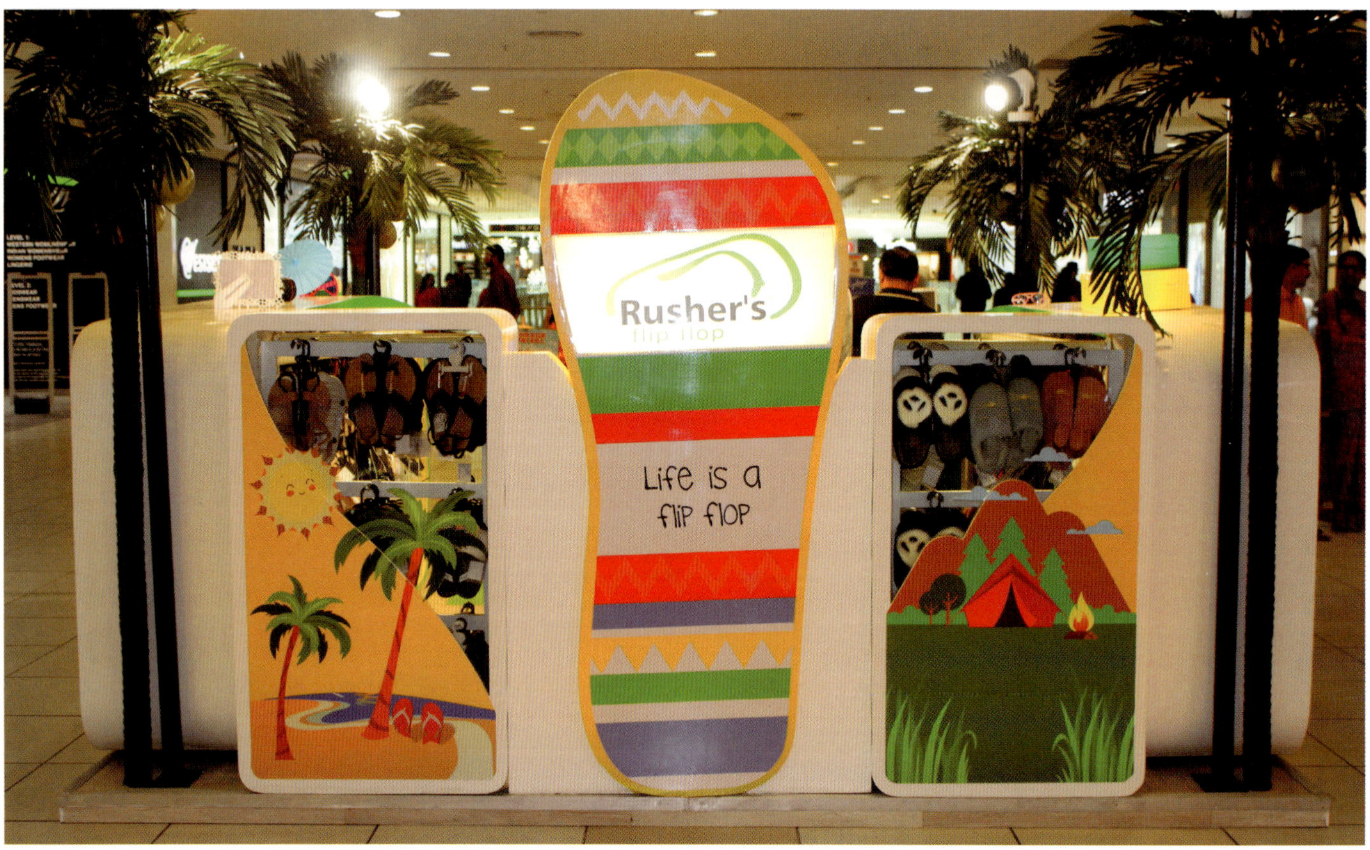

that strike a strong chord with a typical holiday mood at the beach. Most people prefer wearing flip flops at the beach, so we had to build that strong emotional connect and psychological association. People weren't going to buy the product for immediate use, but to use in the future – the next time they were on holiday at the beach.

Discovering

Our team carefully studied the dimensions of the space that the kiosk was to be positioned, including its restrictions and limitations. Functional optimization would have to go hand-in-hand with aesthetic appeal since we had limited space to work within. We drew up a mood board where visual elements were strategically positioned without impeding the high SKU count of the kiosk. Our design methodology would be based on value-sensitive design, incorporating human factors such as lifestyle into the visual fabric.

The Turn

Once we figured out the space optimization, key visual elements that stay true to the brand identity, and cracked the thematic concept, "Holiday Life", the design process for Rusher's Flip Flop was green-lit and good to go. The concept was the most critical part from our perspective, since all communications in terms of both copy and design, would be centered around the concept. It was business-critical to have a concept that was engaging and relatable for the audience.

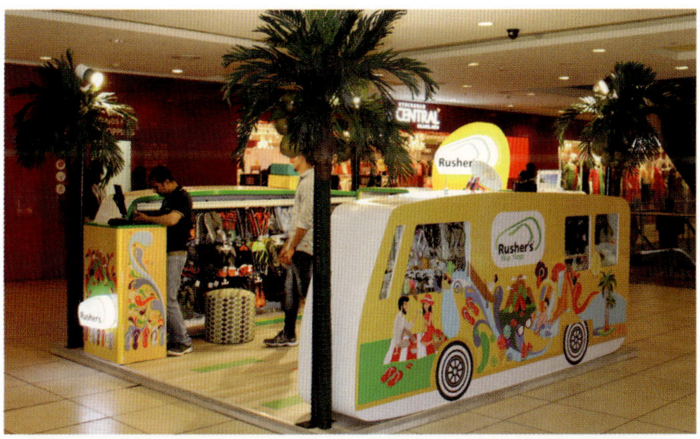

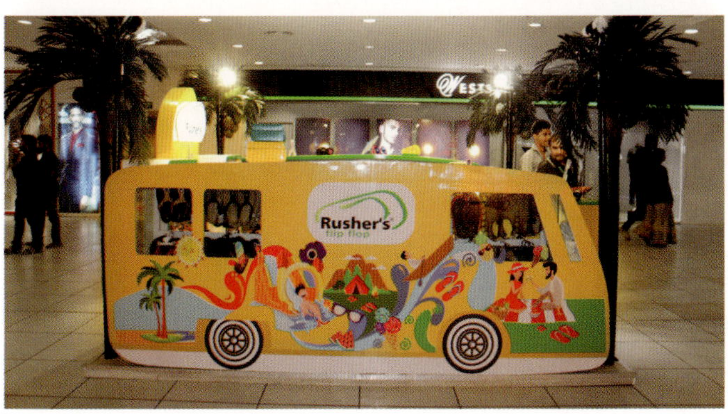

Designing

Coming to the specific details of execution, we had to tailor our design solution to the space allotted in the mall. Our job was to get as many heads to turn and facilitate on-the-spot impulse purchases. We created a "caravan" visual panel blended with the wall fixtures – this turned out to be a visual novelty and a real focal point of attraction.

Delivery

Another key aspect we had to address was security, since the kiosk would be left unguarded after the mall's closing hours. To this end, we incorporated smart, easy pull-down screens with locks to the display units, thereby minimizing the possibility of theft after operational hours. We were able to ensure security of the kiosk in a subtle manner that did not adversely affect the aesthetic appeal of the entire setup.

Looking Back

The kiosk attracted many mall shoppers, and a lot of them ended up making purchases on-the-spot. The increase in footfall also directly led to a sharp increase in brand visibility. This complemented the marketing and business goals of the whole exercise.

Client Speak

"The look-and-feel of the kiosk is excellent. The kiosk is now the mall attraction." Emboldened by success, the client now plans on launching 20 such kiosks across the country.

Landor AXIS BANK

Axis

Card Suite

Agency: Landor
Client: Axis Bank
Category: Visual Communication – Visual Identity

Problem

In an age of virtual bank transactions, the card may be the only physical touch-point we have of a brand. We carry cards 24/7, and yet, as physical objects, they've become uninspiring, and barely stand out in the average purse/wallet. How may the Axis Bank truly stand out from the 'card crowd' and become 'ownably' unique?

Solution

Our idea was to boldly own Axis's signature brand color, Burgundy, one that is ownable and synonymous with the bank. We also aimed to approach every card visually, in order to create highly impactful and styled vignettes of imagery that suggested each card's tiering and benefit. This system is one-of-a-kind and can be expanded to cards in the future. With this opportunity, we aimed to disrupt the market with a clutter-breaking, never-seen-before design system and make the cards become a lifestyle proposition.

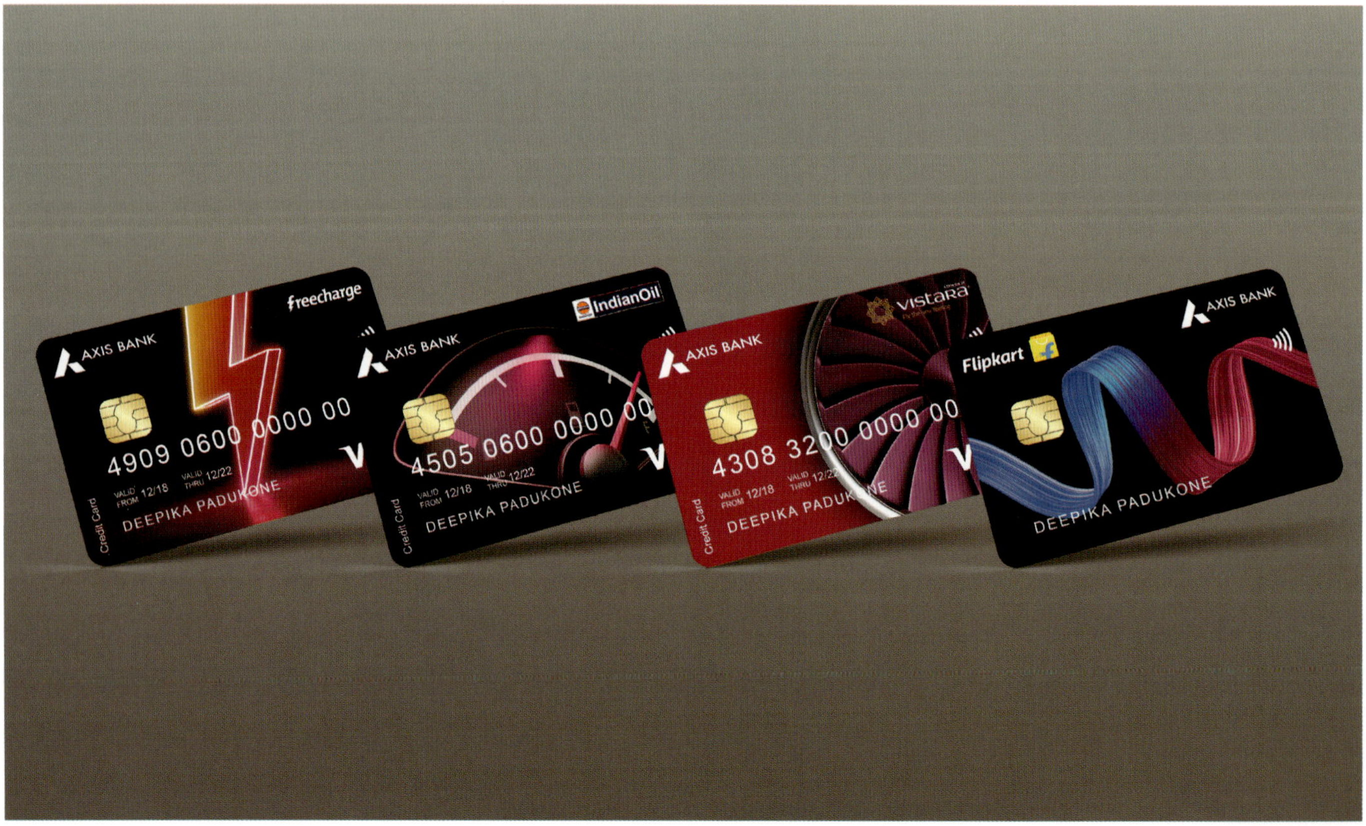

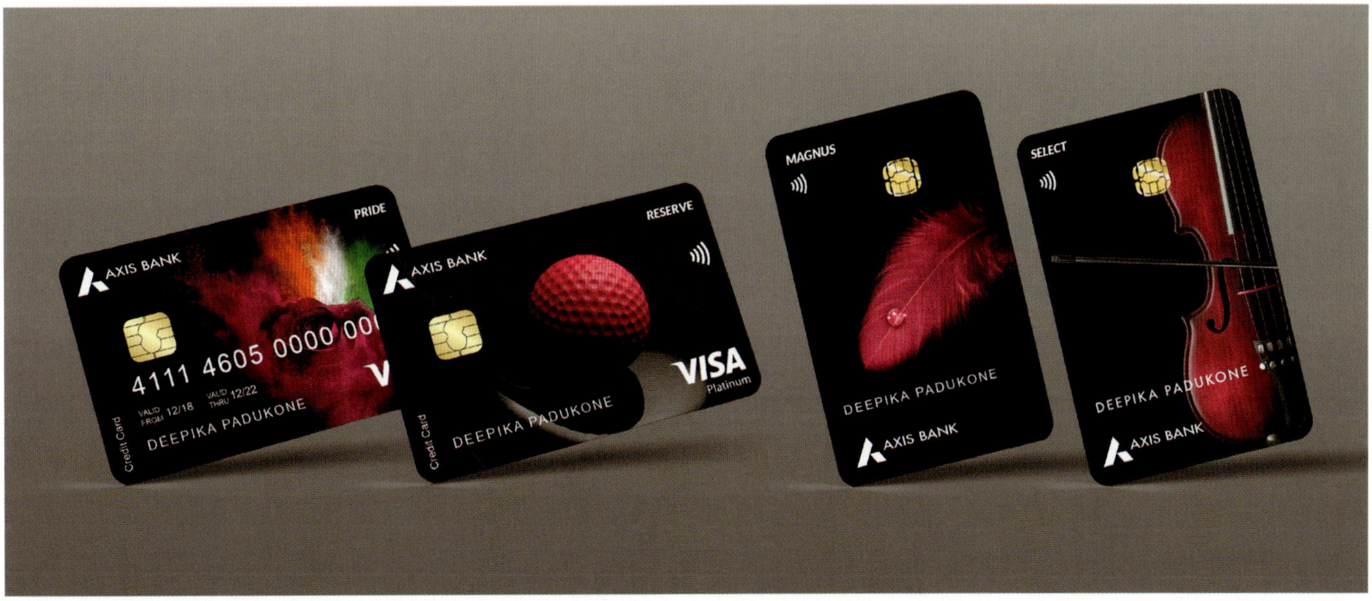
PRIDE
AXIS BANK
4111 4605 0000 00
VALID FROM 12/18
VALID THRU 12/22
DEEPIKA PADUKONE
Credit Card
RESERVE
AXIS BANK
VISA
Platinum
DEEPIKA PADUKONE
Credit Card
MAGNUS
DEEPIKA PADUKONE
AXIS BANK
SELECT
DEEPIKA PADUKONE
AXIS BANK

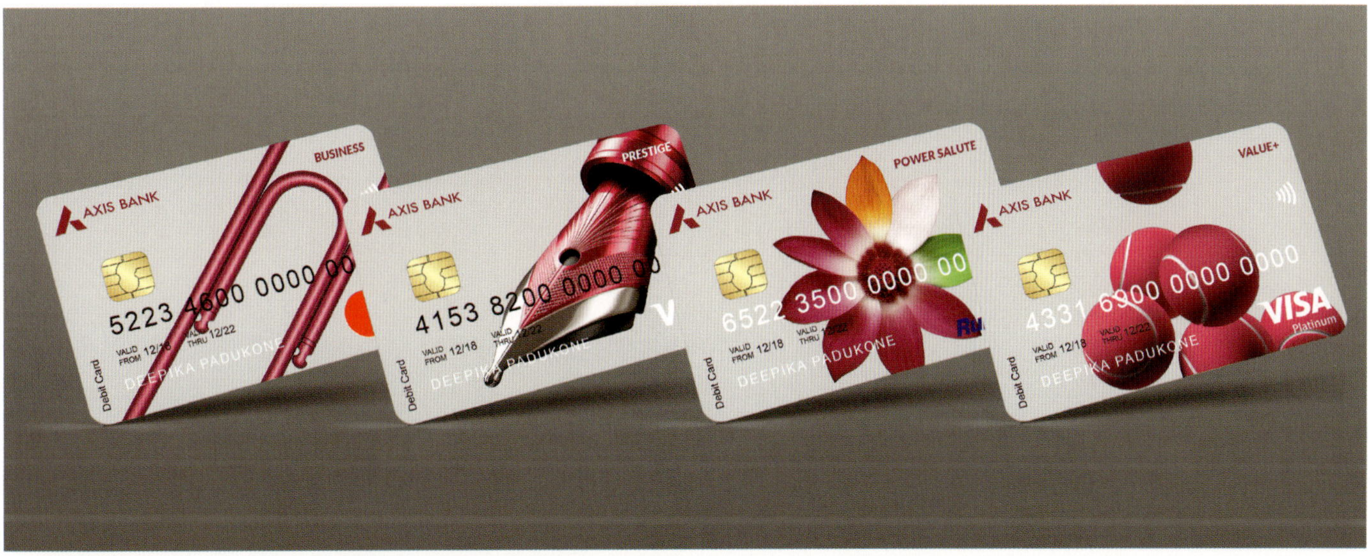
BUSINESS
AXIS BANK
5223 4600 0000 00
Debit Card
PRESTIGE
AXIS BANK
4153 8200 0000 00
Debit Card
POWER SALUTE
AXIS BANK
6522 3500 0000 00
DEEPIKA PADUKONE
Debit Card
VALUE+
AXIS BANK
4331 6900 0000 0000
VISA
Platinum
DEEPIKA PADUKONE
Debit Card

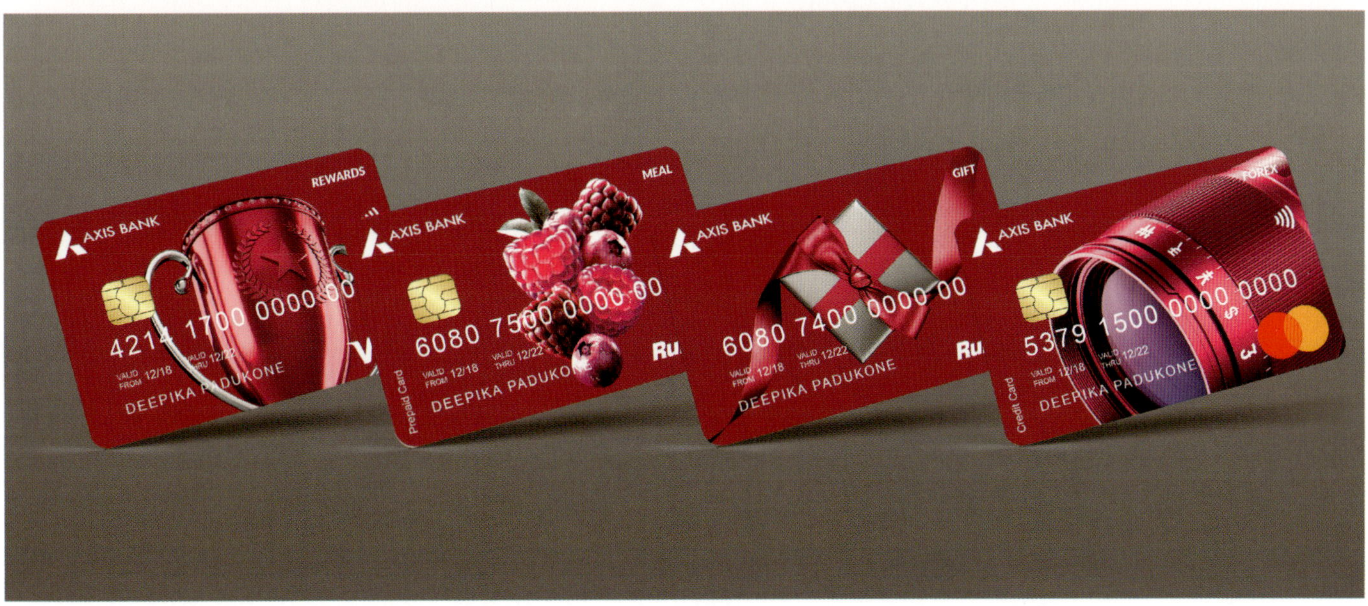
REWARDS
AXIS BANK
4214 1700 0000 00
DEEPIKA PADUKONE
MEAL
AXIS BANK
6080 7500 0000 00
DEEPIKA PADUKONE
Prepaid Card
GIFT
AXIS BANK
6080 7400 0000 00
DEEPIKA PADUKONE
FOREX
AXIS BANK
5379 1500 0000 0000
DEEPIKA PADUKONE
Credit Card

Landor NSE

NSE

Rebranding

Agency: Landor

Client: NSE

Category: Visual Communication – Visual Identity

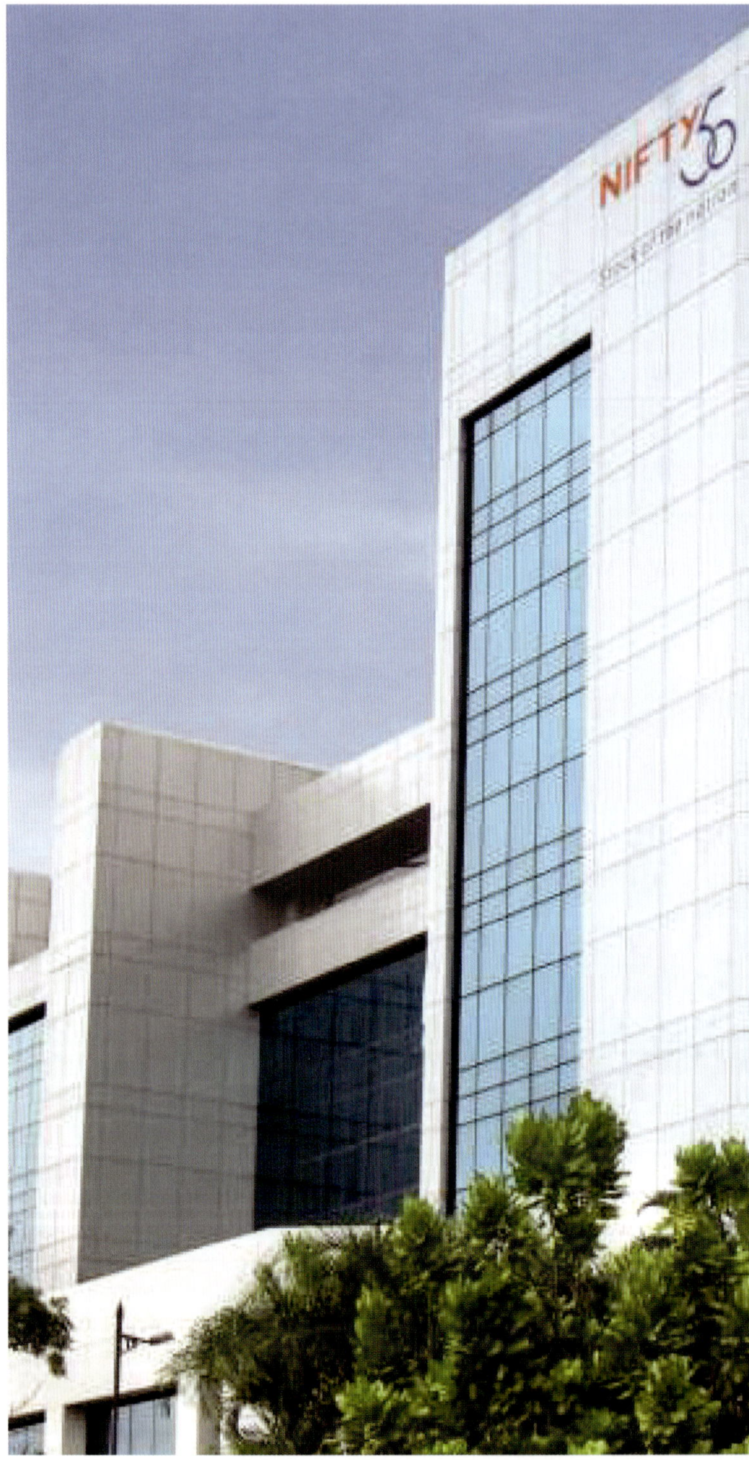

Problem

After more than 25 years of leading the evolution of capital markets in India, the National Stock Exchange of India found itself at a juncture where the speed of change was driving shifts in market conditions, global environments, and peers. As a market leader, NSE wanted to be perceived as more than just a "stock" exchange and be seen instead as an institution focused on driving growth and prosperity in India and globally. There was a strong need for it to be seen as a dynamic and versatile entity, one that is relevant in this digital age of fast moving markets and customers.

Solution

With its massive legacy and widespread impact, at the very core of NSE is its drive to catalyze growth across its stakeholders. We refreshed and strengthened the core of the brand as 'Ambitious for India, Ambitious for You' to reflect its role as a catalyst and partner for India's future growth. We also created a brand expression that is centered around presenting NSE as a platform for agility that is relevant and differentiated. Using the metaphor of a blooming flower, along with a compass that points north, we positioned NSE visually as a brand that is constantly forging ahead, towards a brighter future!

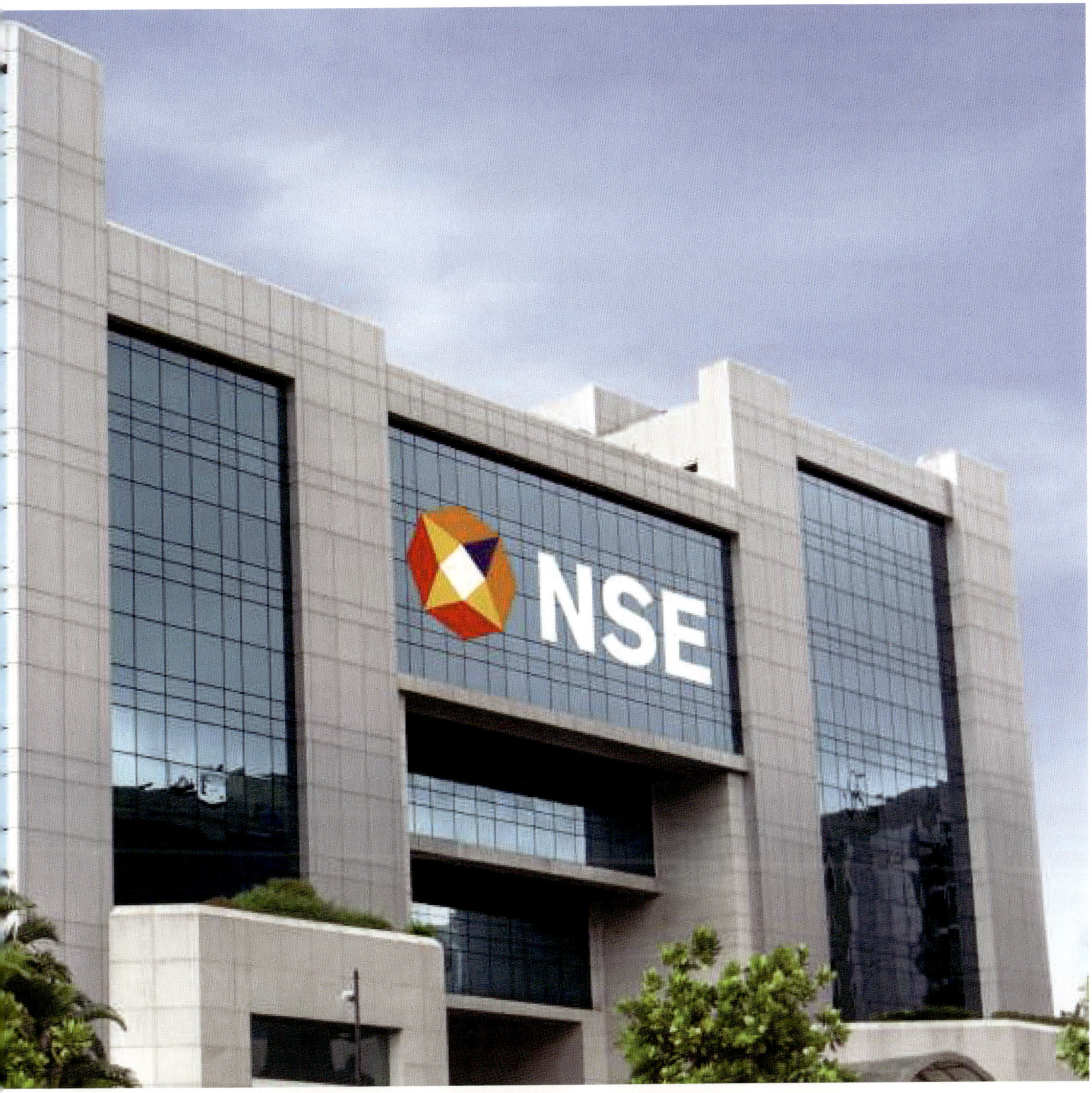
NSE

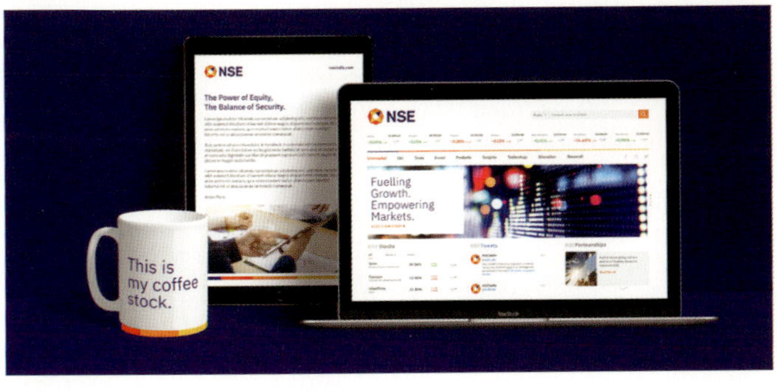
NSE
The Power of Equity,
The Balance of Security.
NSE
Fuelling
Growth.
Empowering
Markets.
This is
my coffee
stock.

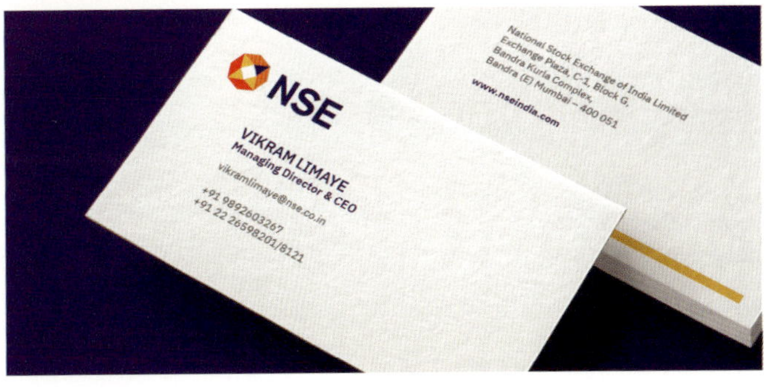
NSE
VIKRAM LIMAYE
Managing Director & CEO
vikramlimaye@nse.co.in
+91 9892603267
+91 22 26598201/8121
National Stock Exchange of India Limited
Exchange Plaza, C-1, Block G,
Bandra Kurla Complex,
Bandra (E) Mumbai - 400 051
www.nseindia.com

Landor

Timepass

Mindless Snacking

Agency: Landor
Client: Britannia Timepass
Category: Visual Communication – Packaging Graphics

Problem

Britannia wanted to enter the challenging USD 34 billion salted snacks category in India. A category characterized by strong competitor brands with massive advertising budgets and a tail of unorganized players. Britannia didn't have the deep pockets its opponents did and wanted to use powerful packaging design as a proxy for media to win market share. Responding to the brief, Landor created a breakthrough design system for Timepass that in six months has disrupted the market leading to a 30 percent rise in customer awareness and 48 percent repeat order rate vis-à-vis competition. Timepass has garnered over 4.5 million social impressions with wafer-thin ad spends.

Solution

Our central idea is based on the observation that snacking is emotionally driven and leads to dramatic changes in facial expressions with every different flavour.

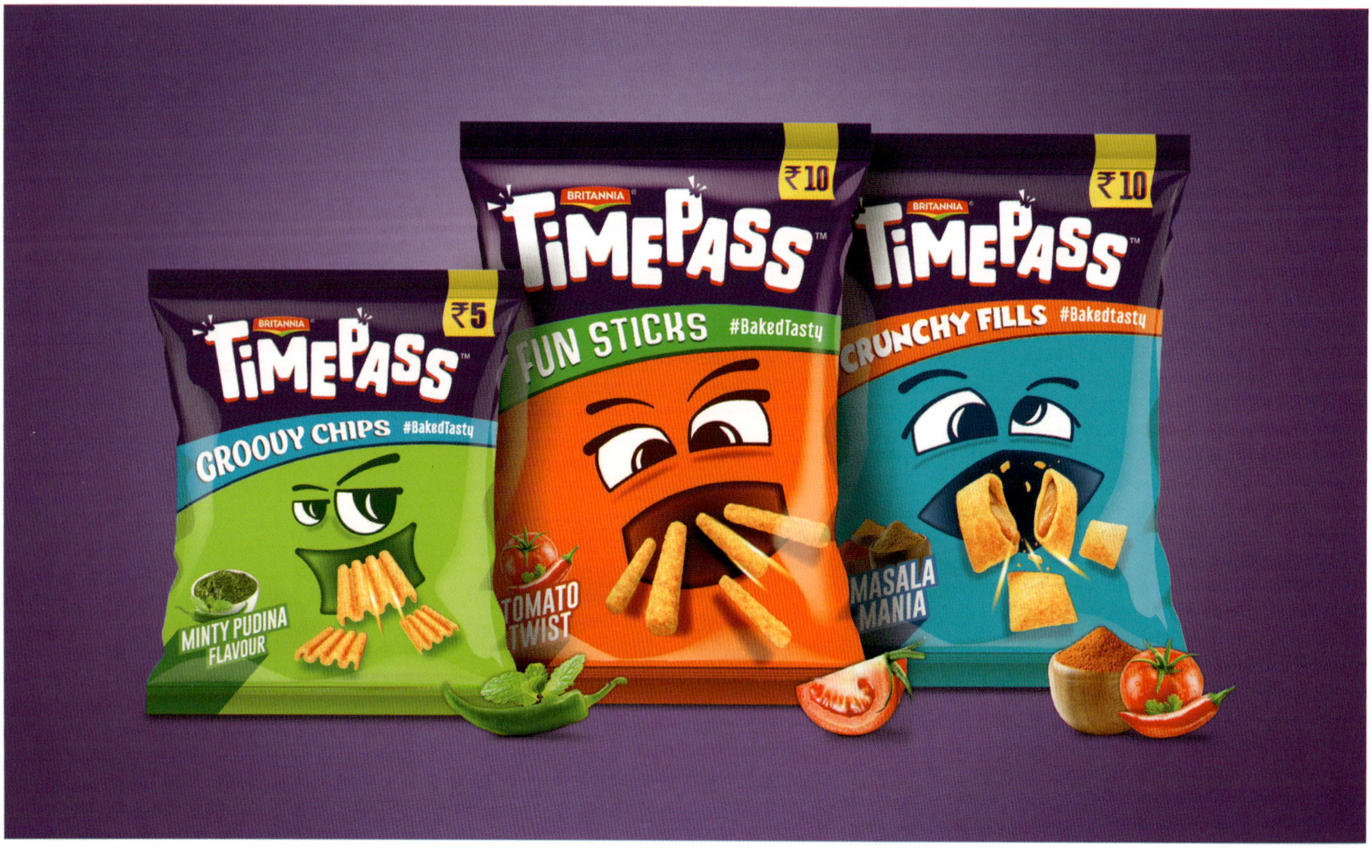

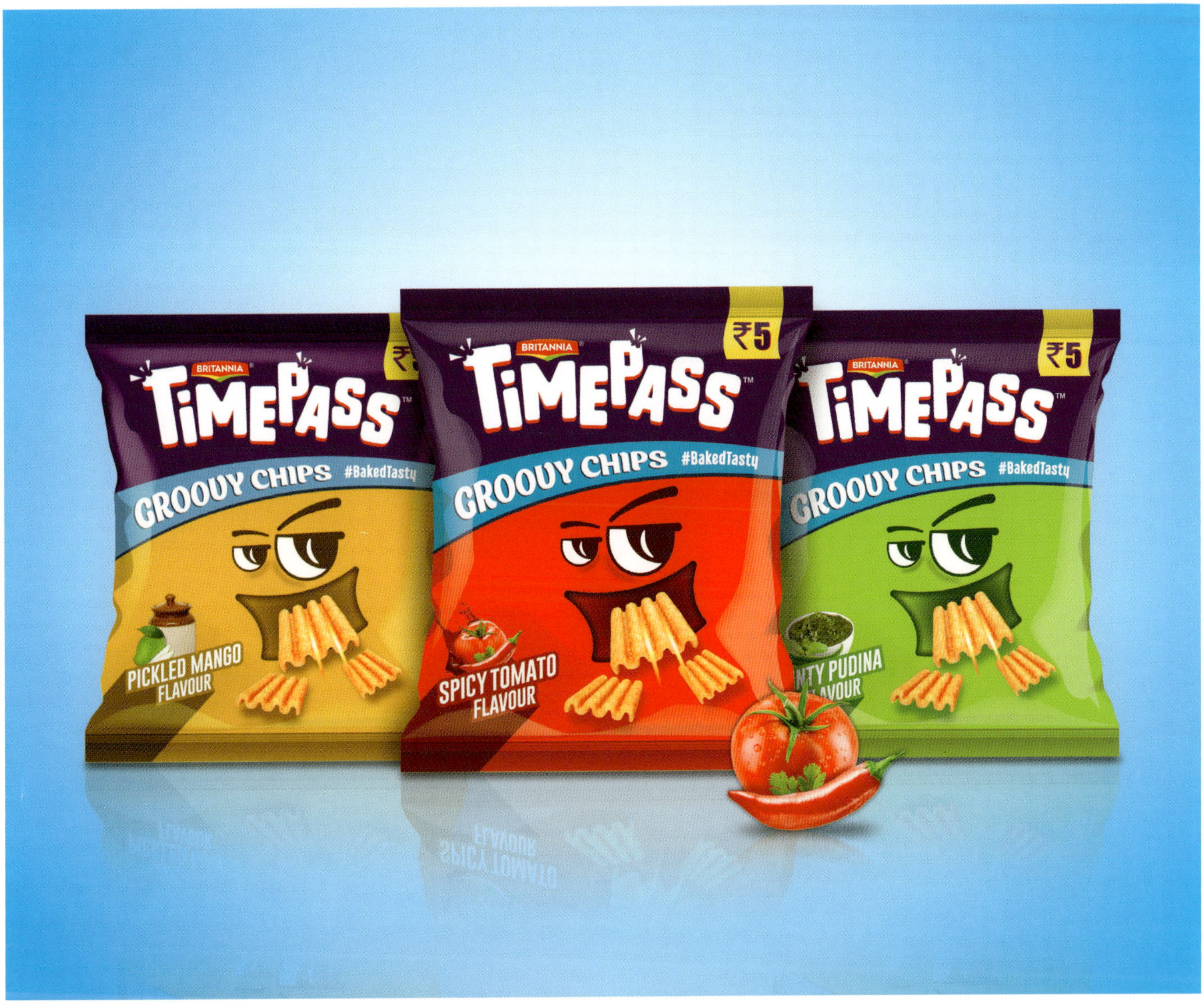
BRITANNIA
TIMEPASS
₹5
GROOVY CHIPS
#BakedTasty
PICKLED MANGO
FLAVOUR
SPICY TOMATO
FLAVOUR

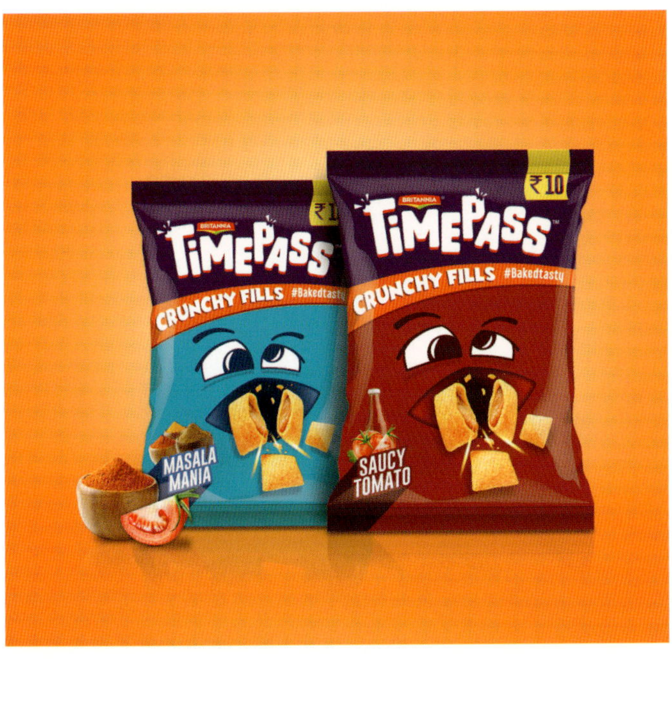
BRITANNIA
TIMEPASS
₹10
CRUNCHY FILLS
#Bakedtasty
MASALA
MANIA
SAUCY
TOMATO

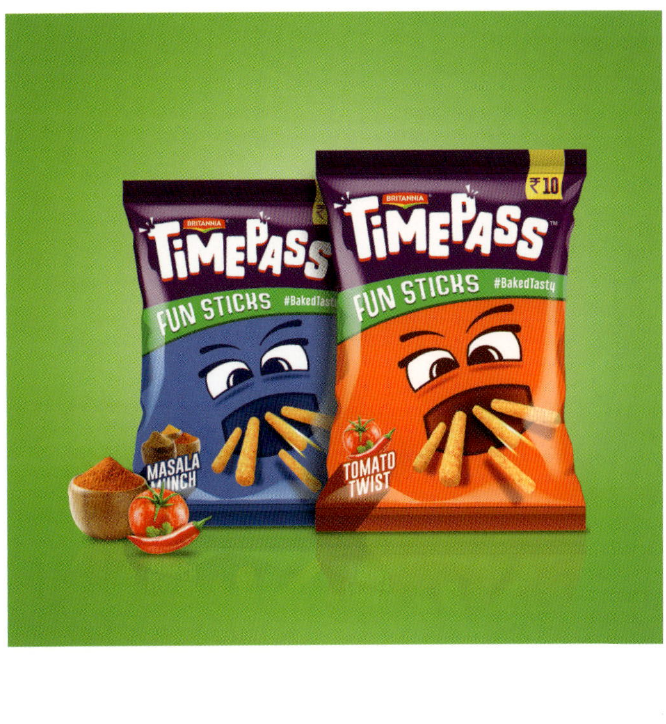
BRITANNIA
TIMEPASS
₹10
FUN STICKS
#BakedTasty
TOMATO
TWIST

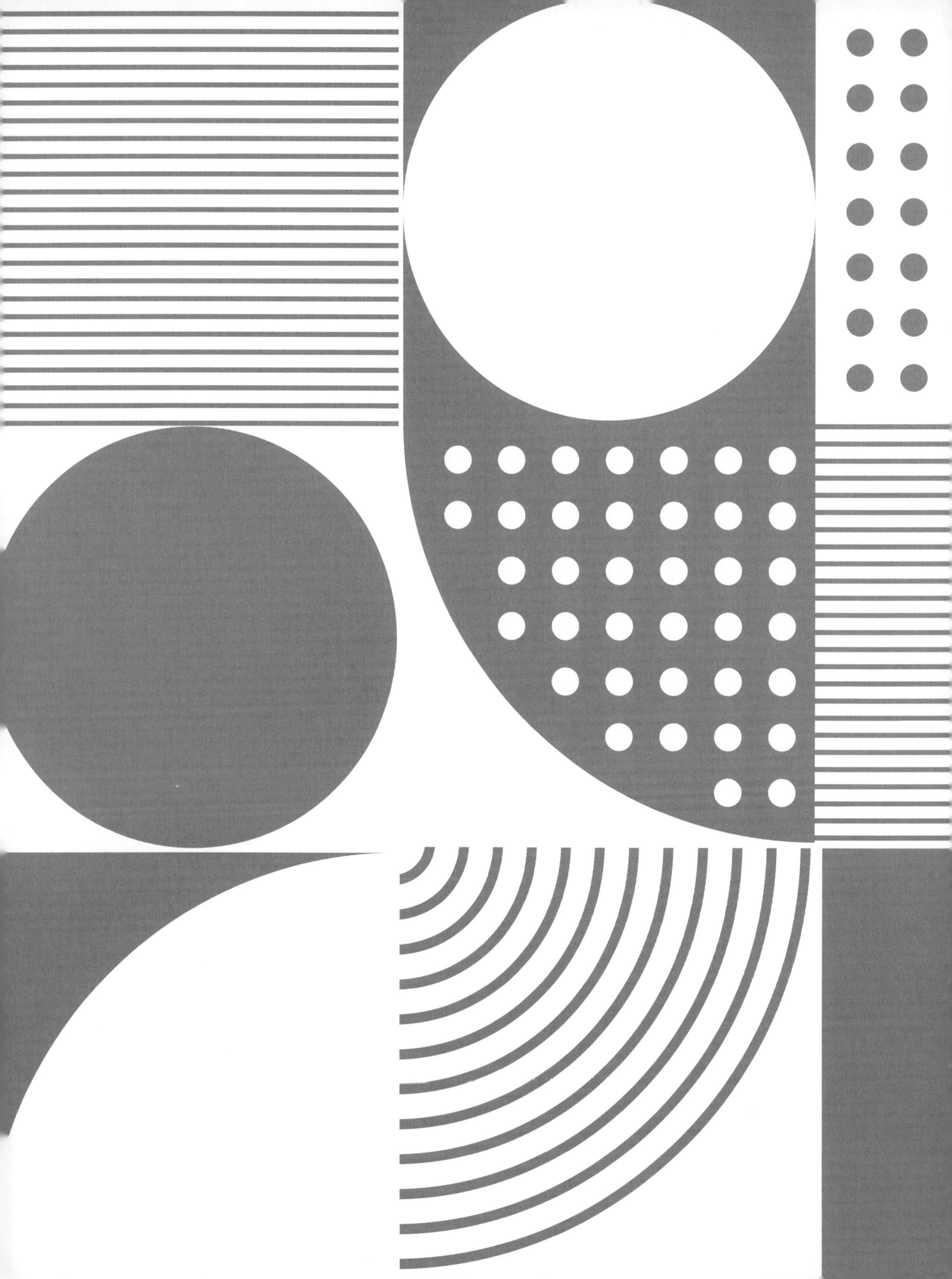

INTERACTION DESIGN

Cumind

An Innovation Platform for CUMI

CONTACT INFORMATION

Company Name: Carborundum Universal Limited

Company Address: 6th floor, Parry House, No. 43, Mooree Strret, Chennai – 600001. Tamil Nadu

Name of Contact Person: Ms Bhavya Kamalia/ Ms Alamelu Pasupathy

Contact Number: +917676444799/+919789482873

Email Address: kamaliab@cumi.murugappa.com/ alamelup@cumi.murugappa.com

Website URL: www.cumind.ooo

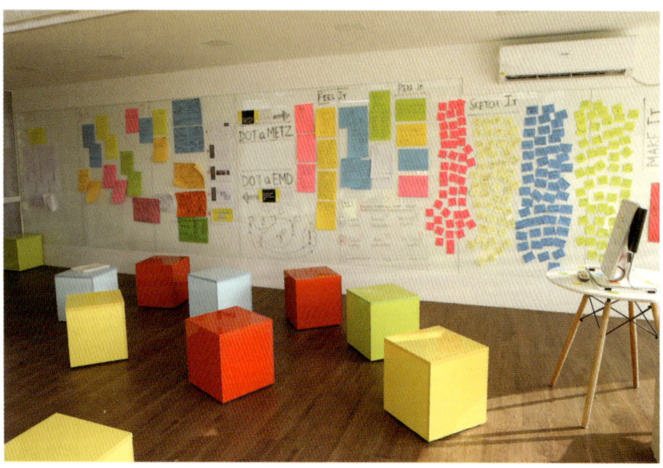

The Problem

Carborundum Universal (CUMI) – A market leader in abrasives and super refractories was looking for a way to create a culture of innovation in their organization. The challenge was to help them evolve an ecosystem that welcomes changes and encourages curiosity.

Assumptions for Design Solutions

It was not just about turning break through ideas into business success, but also about a bigger picture of making the organization innovative by enabling their people to innovate.

The Plan

To arrive at a solution, we designed an experiment called "the journey of an idea". The purpose was to find out how an idea travels in the organizations' ecosystem and where does it end. We conducted a survey across the organization, at all locations, to find the answers.

The first step was to find out that if someone has an idea, can they recognize it? If yes, what do they do? Do they share it casually or on an official channel? Do they work more on it and bring it to a concrete form and pitch it for action? And how does the journey end?

Discovering

We were mostly getting unexperimented thoughts as ideas with minimal backing and, at max, people were just willing to share the idea and not do anything further. We have to make them "do the new" than just "talk the new". We also looked out for other organizations who have solved a similar issue – we studied a few references like Intuit's Catalyst; Adobe's Kickbox. The challenge in this case was the varied user group, starting from the shop-floor employees to the management.

The Turn

A few initial thoughts were like an app for gathering ideas, an idea incubator. But they were not contributing to creating a social behavior, where change and curiosity is welcome. We can't just tell the employees to go forth and innovate.

The idea was to provide them with tools and structures that can demystify innovation and to impart skills that will enable them to use the tools. All this has to happen in the right ambience.

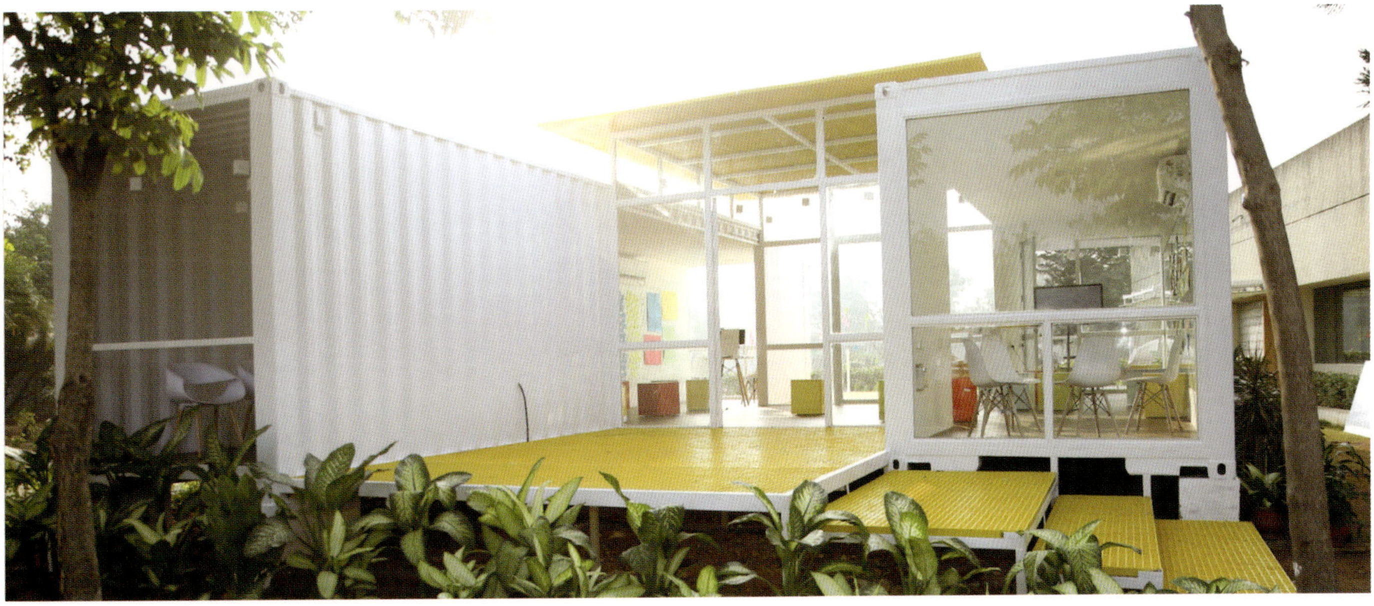

Designing

Cumind was designed with four core offerings: DOT, LOG, ARC and HUB.

- DOT is a framework for solving complex problems through a structured approach, analogous to the one used in design. It is inspired and adopted from the design thinking principles.
- LOG is a device to self-validate ideas and develop them at an individual level. It is inspired by children's learning workbooks.
- ARC is a collection of master classes on necessary skills to innovate. The array of subjects is carefully chosen by observing work-life situation.
- HUB is a "go to" space for innovating minds. Brainstorming spaces, solo work corners, scribble walls and lots of nature are some of the elements of the hub.

Delivery

Inspired by design thinking principles, we designed DOT. We conducted a series of workshops on real problems to standardize it further. And now we have also trained CUMIND champions for each location, who conduct these workshops and foster innovation.

DOT framework has seven steps – "funnel it" – a challenge-identification phase, followed by "feel it, pen it, sketch it, make it, action it" – a series of problem-solving phases, concluded by "stamp it" – where the solution is incorporated into their daily worklife.

LOG enables employees to explore ideas at an individual level and ARC classes were design to impart skills.

In HUB, the creative ambience was created using upcycled shipping containers. The vibrant interiors were made flexible, with glass-cladded walls for scribbling, rotating table that you can write on for brain-storming, moving cube stools, interactive touch-screen monitors, sit-outs for discussion, among others.

Looking Back

The plan is to create one hub at each factory location and to make people use the tools effectively. Once we use the tools and apply the learnings, they tend to evolve more. As the culture develops, we also look forward to adding more verticals as and when needed.

CUMIND is developed to make continuous innovation possible. We have put in processes, trained teams and a have created a place for people to ideate and innovate as a collective team. With this, we look forward to creating a culture of innovation.

ICICI Bank

Instabanking – ICICI Bank

CONTACT INFORMATION

Company Name: ICICI Bank

Company Address: ICICI Bank Tower, Ground Floor, Bandra Kurla Complex, Mumbai - 400051

Name of Contact Person: M. Balaji

Contact Number: +91 9004246662

Email Address: balaji.m@icicibank.com

Website URL: www.icicibank.com

The Problem

InstaBanking is an initiative by ICICI Bank the second largest bank in the country to further reduce dependency on humans to carry out transactions. It works at two levels, you can initiate a transaction which involves going to bank through a mobile and also walk into any of the InstaBanking kiosks and carry out your activities without any help. This has allowed ICICI bank to expand its physical footprint without the need of recruitment in deep down areas of the country. The task was was to revamp this old legacy system to a more modern and usable interface.

Assumptions for Design Solutions

Since InstaBanking is going to be ever-evolving service, it was important for us to build an architecture that would live with the times. Agility and nimbleness was one of the prime requirements from the project which was delivered through modular approach toward the UI.

The Plan

The KIOSK was planned to reflect a modern interface with learnings from mobility ICICI bank kiosk now natively leverages touch-usability guidelines as opposed to website to ease out the users.

The whole idea of augmenting technology to deliver banking services in deep-down regions is an innovative one. It required the whole team to think in parallel paths to deliver the solution. On the one hand, we wanted modernism and ease of use, on the other hand we had handle multilingual capabilities and lastly, it had to be agile.

Discovering

Going to deep-down areas of the country also means being ready to adapt the interface in different languages. The kiosk currently features three languages—English, Hindi, and Marathi—which covers around 40 per cent of the population. The aim is to roll out the services in 11 languages. The new architecture allows the bank to quickly adopt the languages.

The overall time during research spent by any user was approximately 2–3 minutes which was essentially due to lag in finding service and bad screen usability. With the new interface, we were able to bring that down to 30 seconds which helped in reducing the queue at these kiosks and hence became more approachable.

The Turn

This project worked in a completely reverse mentality. It was stripped down to bare minimum to drive adoption. Since time spent in the bank had to be reduced, we looked at a model which will effectively deliver on that.

Stripping the app down to bare minimum allowed users to quickly decipher the screen architecture and quickly move forward. This also saw an increase in the trust that

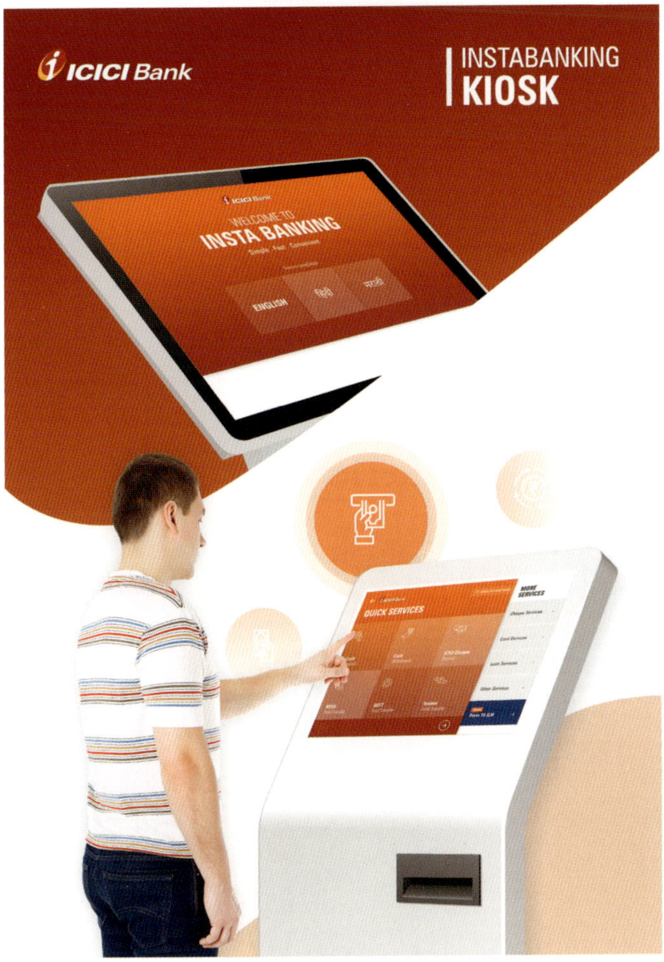

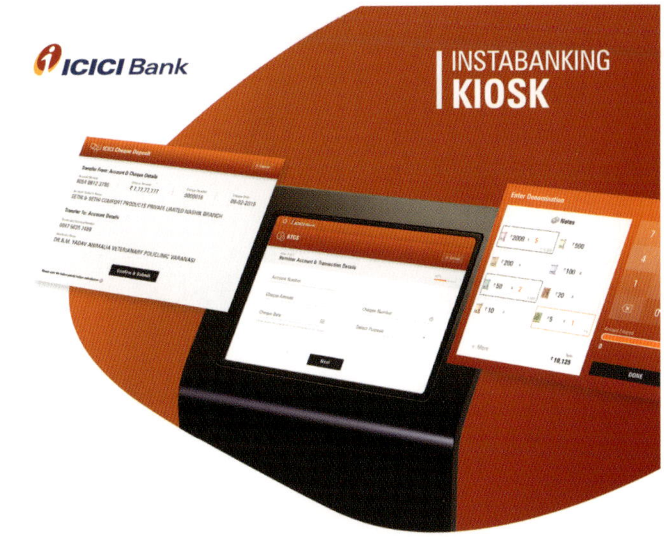

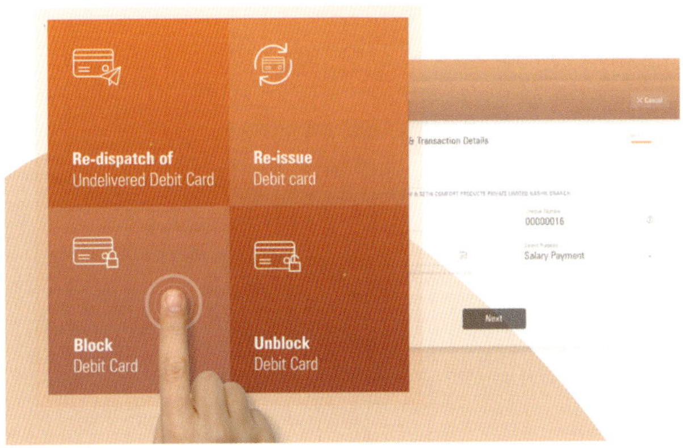

bank officials had with this, which meant that they actively started marketing this product internally in their branches.

Designing

Getting the design of Instabanking Kiosk right was not a choice. It was a key ingredient in ICICI's customer satisfaction matrix for people walking into the branch. The design process was a bit unique in this case as opposed to traditional. We looked at customer touchpoints in various retail outlets where the key intent was to get out as soon as possible. We took clues from places such as petrol pumps, airports, box office, where kiosks were serving some of the needs. When we analyzed these services, we saw that kiosks are approached in a specific scenario and only used for a focused set of services. This allowed us to use the data and cut down on experiences that we needed to build. This discovery lead a lean product with much better outcome overall.

Looking Back

The steep increase in the usage of InstaBanking kiosk after the launch of the new interface is a testimony to its success. Also we saw fewer errors during the cash deposit cycle where people got frustrated by counting the wrong denominations and had to restart the process. This, apparently, was a big relief to them where the design allowed them to rectify mistake instantly.

Client Speak

"Instabanking Kiosk is one of the key components of ICICI bank brick-and-mortar infrastructure. With help of Fractal Ink, we were able to turn around the experience of this artefact and made it more relevant. Today we are able to drive a sizeable transaction within the bank through this intervention." – M Balaji, Product Head, ICICI bank.

FRACTAL INK
Linked by isobar EXPERIENCE DESIGN AND CONSULTANCY

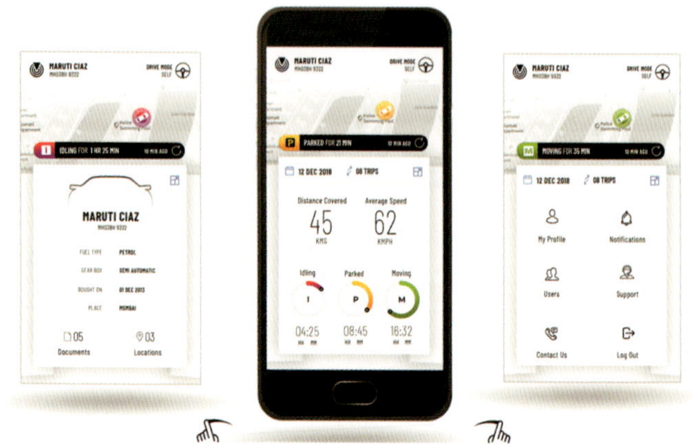

Matchpoint GPS-Connected App

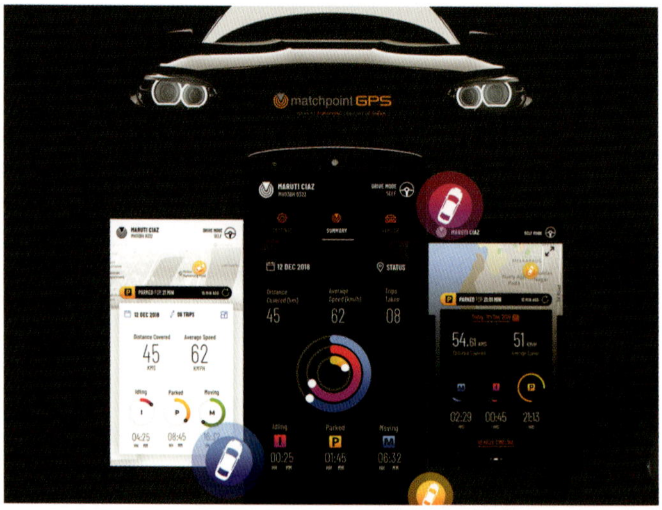

CONTACT INFORMATION

Company Name: Matchpoint GPS Pvt. Ltd.

Company Address: Lotus Corporate Park, B-Wing, Office No. 1702, 1801 & 1802, Western Express Hwy, Goregaon, Mumbai

Name of Contact Person: Devang Goradia

Contact Number: +91 9821732223

Email Address: devang@matchpointgps.com

Website URL: https://matchpointgps.com/

The Problem

Matchpoint GPS vehicle-tracking solution is India's most valuable, comprehensive and affordable connected car solution for consumers with the largest customer base in the country. Whenever you embark on a domain that's relatively new, the biggest challenge is around benchmarking. Matchpoint GPS is a new and emerging segment. For us the goal was to not only design the experience but also establish a benchmark in the industry. Fractal ink was entrusted to help matchpoint GPS design the user experience for their consumer-facing applications.

Assumptions for Design Solutions

Tracking your car data is a fairly new concept in India and when such a problem statement arises, usually we start with lot of intuition. Here one of the biggest assumptions was that people are looking out for the kind of data we are churning. Since there is no precedence, it was a make-or-break for the product.

The Plan

The customer experience was thought from bottom-up philosophy. With loads of data being collected, it became important for us to carefully map them into a hierarchy so that users don't get overwhemlmed with it. Since a lot of information that the hardware collected was unknown to the users till date, it was important for us to not flaunt it mindlessly.

Matchpoint GPS puts a hierarchy matrix over all its data and presents it to the users in the most meaningful order. It has also taken care that the most basic and essential information pops up without any effort with an ability to drill down. This progressive learning helps audience to quickly get used to the app, and then allows time to learn deep functionalities.

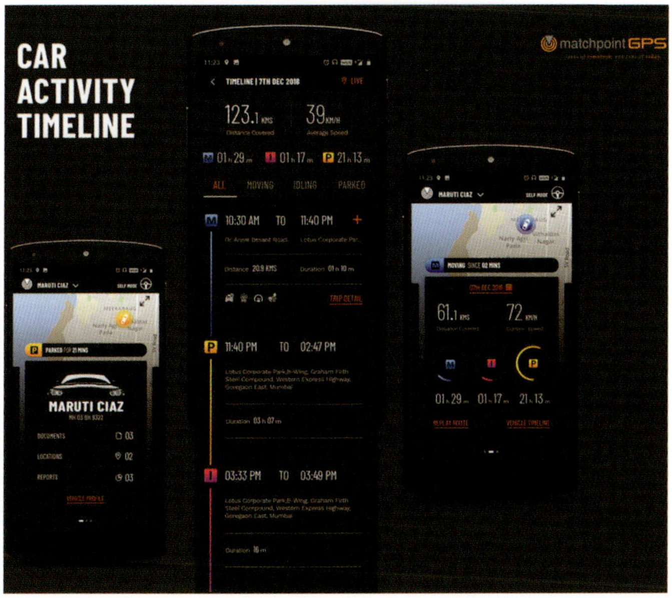

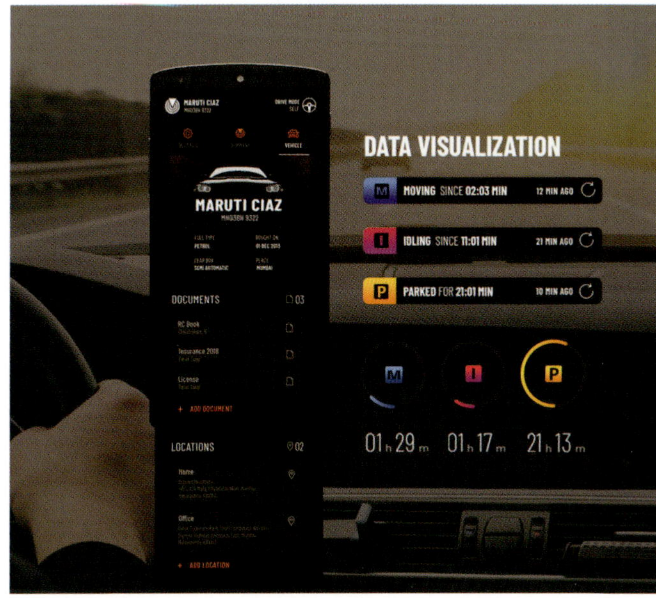

Discovering

We conducted a primary research to understand the current acceptance of the app and tried building up hypothesis which resounds with the feedback. The discovery process helped us to map data and build algos which are meaningful for a common person to understand and have a take away.

The Turn

The automobile industry is one of the fastest changing segment around us. From self-driven cars to smart cars, the way we interact with one of our most prized possession is changing fast.

In today's day and age, data is key to any organization's success. But merely collecting data and throwing it up to the users is a bad idea. When we looked at data and saw the insight it can provide for the users, it changed the we way looked at cars altogether. Matchpoint GPS was able to put a hierarchy matrix over all its data and present it to the users in the most meaningful order.

It's also taken care that the most basic and essential information pops up without any effort with an ability to drill down.

Designing

This progressive learning helps audience to quickly get used to the app and then allows time to learn deep functionalities. This called for developing a system which is agile and growing. This system will perfect itself over time and help people build their habits along. We also built strong UI associations which are friendly to all groups of people so that going ahead, it shouldn't conflict with any other system and becomes a standard of its own.

Looking Back

Every new domain brings a new aspect to our journey. Apart from learning from the domain, we were able to expand our vision to IOT products. While automobile automation is not new we saw how context and geography affects product development.

Client Speak

"Working with Fractal Ink was a great learning for our teams as well. Being a development company, sometimes technology blinds us, but the way Fractal articulated the user stories and brought data to life was amazing."
–Devang Goradia, CTO

FRACTAL INK
Linked by isobar EXPERIENCE DESIGN AND CONSULTANCY

Shemaroo Entertainment Digital Ecosystem

CONTACT INFORMATION

Company Name: Shemaroo Pvt. Ltd

Company Address: Plot No. 18, Shemaroo House, Off Andheri Kurla Road, Marol Co-Op Ind Estate, Phase 18, Andheri East, Mumbai.

Name of Contact Person: Zubin Dubash

Contact Number: +91 9223256749

Email Address: zubin.dubash@shemaroo.com

Website URL: https://www.shemarooent.com/

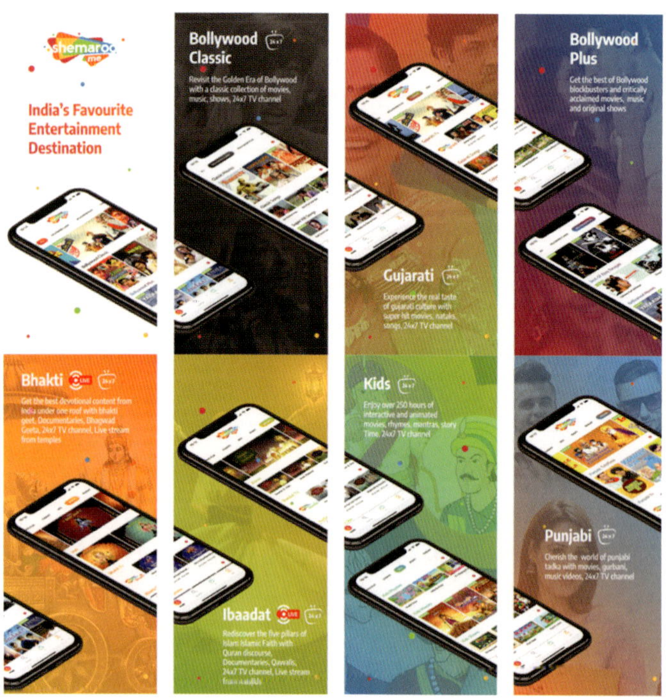

The Problem

Shemaroo Entertainment Limited has made its mark in the Indian entertainment industry by being one of the oldest players in content ownership, aggregation and distribution. With a collection of more than 3,700 movie titles, they offer services to customers across the globe. Fractal Ink was brought on board to create Shemaroo's OTT platform, ShemarooMe. The platform would be available on web, smartphone and TV.

Assumptions for Design Solutions

Lack of original Indian content was a big driver for Shemaroo to embark upon this journey. With strong assumptions that there is a need for Indian audience across the globe to build something which is reflective of our culture, taste and viewing habits, we developed this app to be completely Indian in nature.

The Plan

Having no independent digital presence before, it was a challenge for the Fractal team to create a complete OTT experience, across multiple devices, in a span of 2 months. To tackle the challenge in the best way possible, the team worked towards creating a platform that took the classics of Indian entertainment and brought them alive through a modern and minimalist interface. The team made the best of the two months and created an all-round OTT experience that looked appealing and ranked high in terms of usability.

Discovering

Designing the subscription model entails a holistic understanding of the consumers' thought process. Based on research, there is an evident difference in the content consumption of the local and international Indian viewers of Shemaroo. Hence, the Fractal team customized separate journeys for both the target segments.

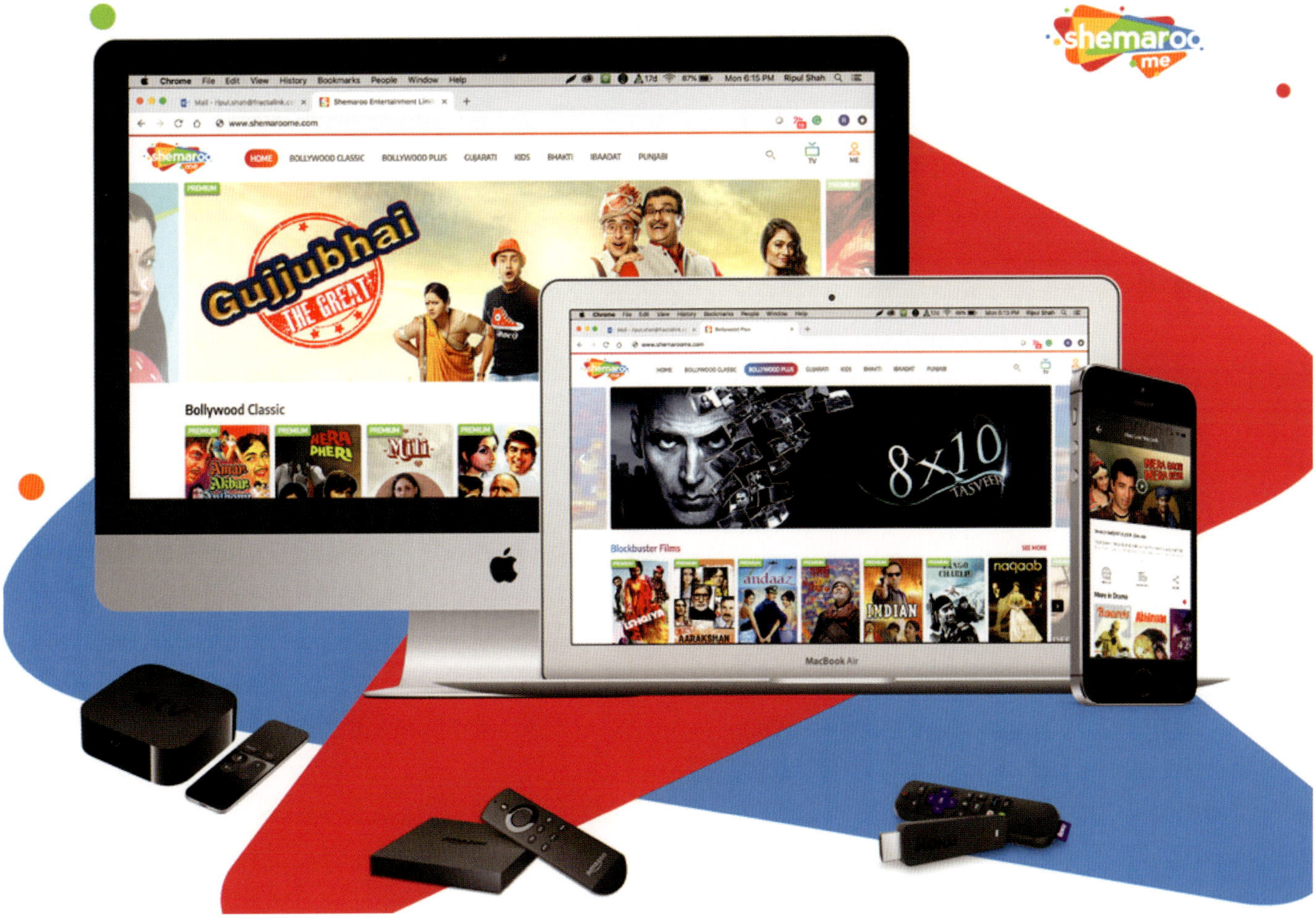

The Turn

Being a content aggregator has its advantages and ShemarooMe was built on the app with content exclusive to the Indian audience, the design aimed at highlighting exclusivity in all its inclusiveness.

ShemarooMe has created independent channels which stream their content and this is exclusive to the premium users on web and app. They are made to increase awareness of different programmes as well as drive viewership for similar content based on user preferences.

Designing

This progressive learning helps audience to quickly get used to the app and then allows time to learn deep functionalities. This called for developing a system which is agile and growing. This system will perfect itself over time and help people build their habits along. We also built strong UI associations which are friendly to all groups of people so that going ahead it shouldn't conflict with any other system and becomes a standard of its own

Looking Back

We were able to deliver a platform which had a distinctive look and proposition in the otherwise crowded market. Also, we helped Shemaroo discover its new identity in the digital era which helped strengthen its position in the industry

Client Speak

"Fractal Ink has been phenomenal in transforming this vision into reality. With the strong experience in OTT platforms they were able to early on guide us in defining certain ground rules of transforming content into digital. The diligence, speed and output of the fractal team was phenomenal." –Zubin Dubash, Chief Digital Officer

FRACTAL INK
Linked by isobar
EXPERIENCE DESIGN AND CONSULTANCY

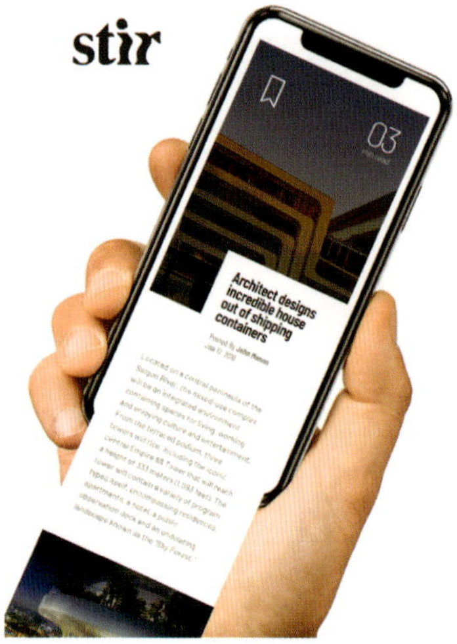

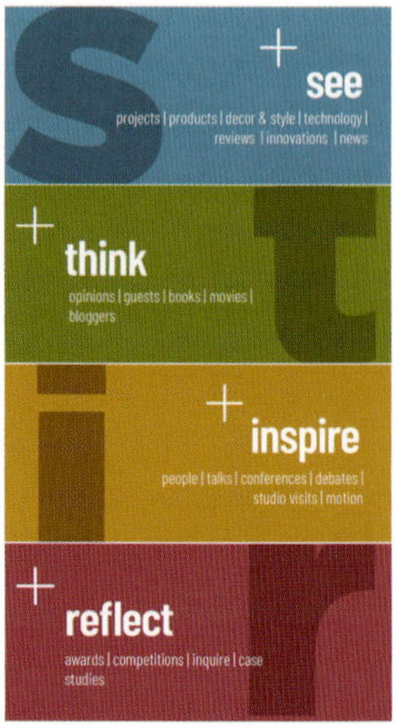

STIR

Rediscovering the Brand

CONTACT INFORMATION

Company Name: STIR Design Private Limited

Company Address: DLF Chattarpur Farms, 2, North Dr, Chhatarpur

Name of Contact Person: Amit Gupta

Contact Number: +91 9811128344

Email Address: amit@stirdesign.in

Website URL: https://www.stirworld.com/

The Problem

When you have an iconic brand, which has its strong presence around, it becomes extremely challenging to reimagine it. STIR is a popular name with strong values which people associate with. One of the biggest challenges was how to create something which immediately resonates and forms a part of the memory.

With established eyes from the field of art, architecture and design looking at this brand closely, Fractal had this humungous challenge to design something equally iconic which would trigger conversations in this highly judgemental community in a positive light.

Assumptions for Design Solutions

Internet is overloaded with content and we see most of them feeling similar.

When we designed the digital avatar for STIR, the idea was to harness the design language and continue pushing the boundary. We came up with some rather unique representation of pictures and typography which helped us get that refreshing look.

It did involve a lot of curation and a keen eye while putting together the content, but who said quality comes easily.

STIR is a refreshing content platform which does justice to the content and elevates the communication.

The Plan

Sometimes a disciplined process towards design helps build a strong foundation for brand design.

- **Research:** We started out by studying the current brand, its standing in the market and its perception.
- **Brainstorming and Conceptualization:** The concept was put to test at various stages to understand its impact. It was blown up scaled down to understand if it lives up to the visual grind.
- **Implementation:** The final implementation involved creating the logo unit and coming up with the brand language which can speak in its own grammar to the audience.

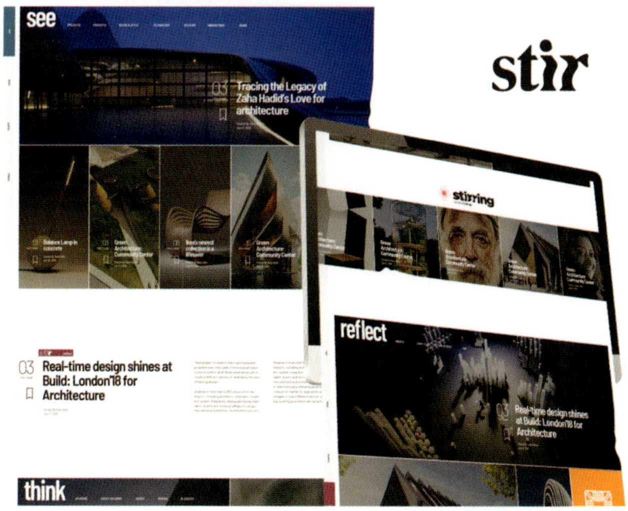

Discovering

Instituted in 2014, STIR was founded to promote, propagate and foster creativity and innovation in the fields of design, architecture and interactive art in India and across the world. In 2015, STIR launched its first initiative, "mondo*arc india", a content-led and perspective-driven publication that soon become the country's fastest growing design journal. It garnered popular acclaim as "the well-read design magazine" and enjoyed an unmatched reputation among professionals, students and enthusiasts alike. STIR today manifests into a global platform for content creation and consumption specializing in architecture, design and art.

Fractal Ink was trusted to create a new identity for STIR and strategies the online journey for them.

The Turn

The eureka moment happened when one of our designers defined Stir as something which is path-breaking ... something like a hurricane that clears path for something new.

That was the birth if STIR we created a non-perfect form which not only encapsulated the emotion of path-breaking but also gave it an identity which stood out among other brands.

The result was a memorable differentiated and an iconic symbol whose deformation became the identity.

Designing

Many a times we design something because we like it and it looks good. Which is fair. But, over a period, we are left with great dissonance between the brand and what the organization is doing. This is usually because the foundation of brand design was shallow. We, at STIR, aimed for building a system which allows the organization to grow over a period of time making sure that their identity is intact.

Right from building a library of artefacts to building usage scenarios was a part of Fractal's responsibilities. We ensured that not only is the brand seen differently but also the experience is consistent with the brand's visual manifestation.

Looking Back

The impact was an overwhelming response from the crowd at the launch. The design community applauded to this unusual approach and definitely termed it as a path-breaking approach in the field of identity design.

The brand identity embraced deformity as a challenge and brought it alive in various artefacts. The treatment of the images, stationary, and brand elements reiterated the beauty in the irregular-ness – a true reflection of how an identity can become a language for an institution. Each of the brand elements was able to reflect the emotion and create a memory among the audience which was a win for us.

Client Speak

"Working with Fractal Ink on the STIR rebranding has been one of the most exciting project in the recent times. It was great to have a design team alongside your journey who are as much passionate about design as us. STIR's new brand is truly a reflection of who we want to be."
–Amit Gupta, Founder Director

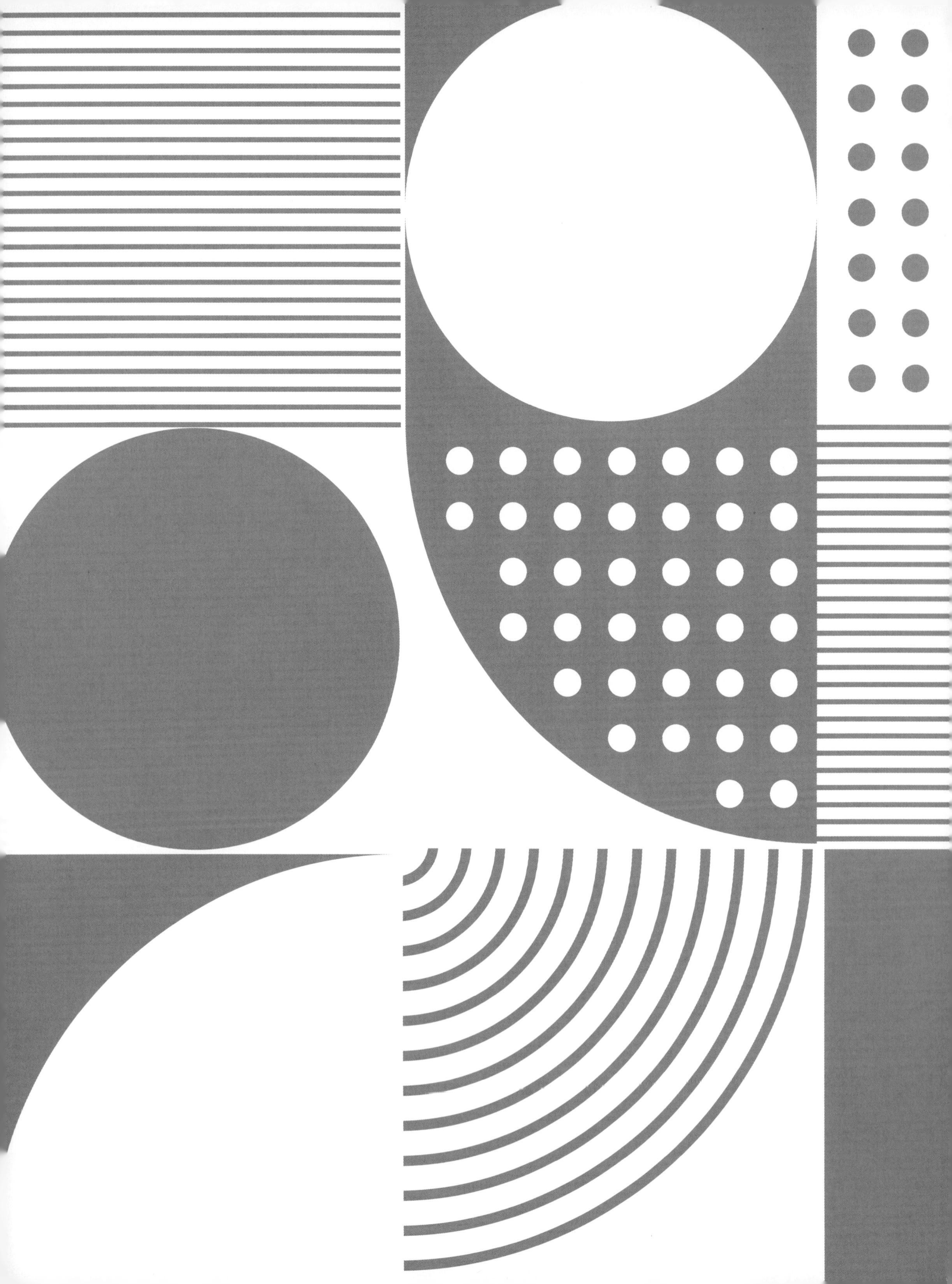

MOBILITY
DESIGN

ABHIKALP
DESIGN STUDIO

Abhikalp Design Studio

Premium Electric City Bus

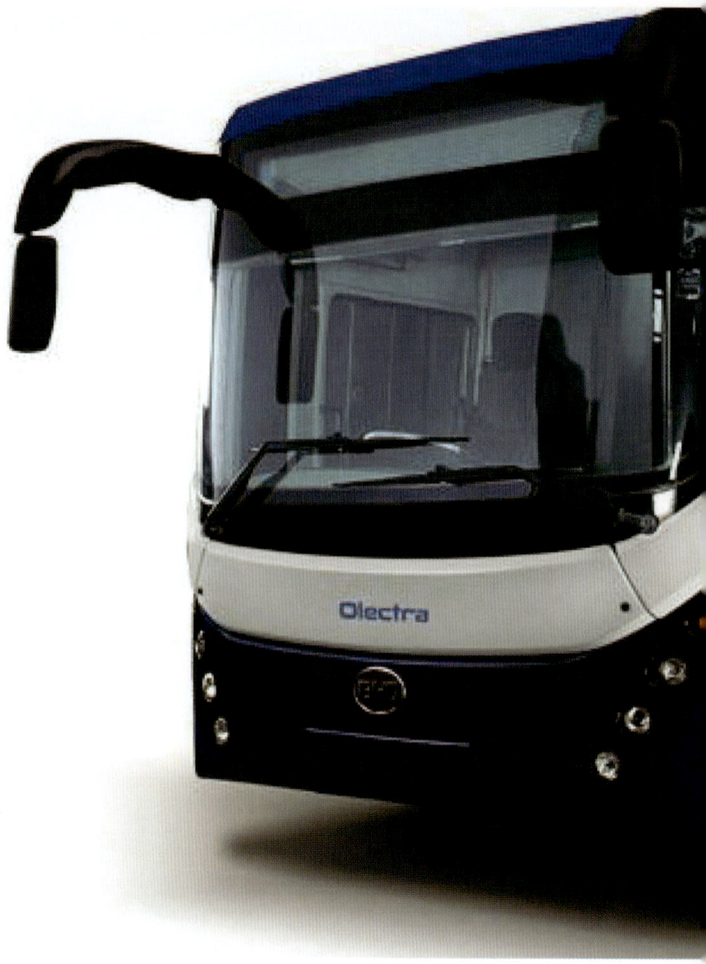

CONTACT INFORMATION
Company Name: Olectra Greentech Ltd
Company Address: Center Point Building, 4th Floor,Plot No.359 to 363/401, Begumpet, Secunderabad – 500 016, Telangana.
Name of Contact Person: Mr Anil Bhan, President
Contact Number: +91 9100699907
Email Address: anil.bhan@olectra.com
Website URL: www.olectra.com

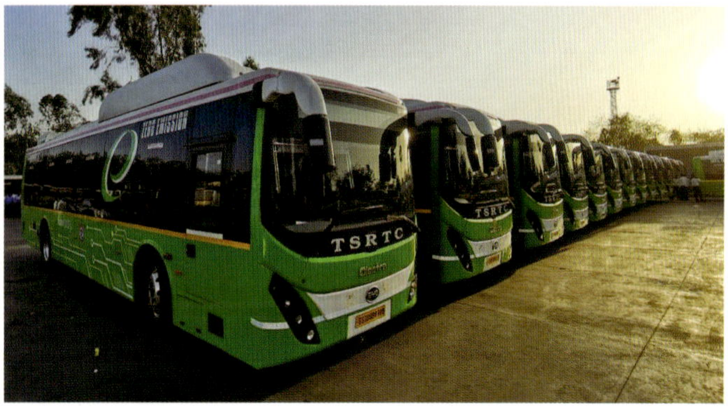

The Problem

Considering the congested and polluted roads of Indian cities, a premium electrically operated non-polluting mass-transport city bus system is required which can offer aspirational values to the commuters and de-congesting the available infrastructure. As the Indian government is giving more emphasis on electric vehicles, the next automobile boom lies in the electric vehicles only.

Assumptions for Design Solutions

BYD-China is the world leader in electric bus manufacturing with proven technology. Thus, the first assumption is taken that the proven technology will work very well in India, which is backed up by the Indian technology partner Olectra Greentech Ltd. The second assumption has been the development of vehicle charging ecosystem backed by the positive thrust of the Indian Government for electric mobility.

The Plan

Olectra-BYD needed the city buses to cater to metropolitan cities as well as smaller Indian cities with limited road infrastructure. The business model defined the requirement of bus solutions to be run by municipal corporations and transport societies along with the complete ecosystem. This way only the business

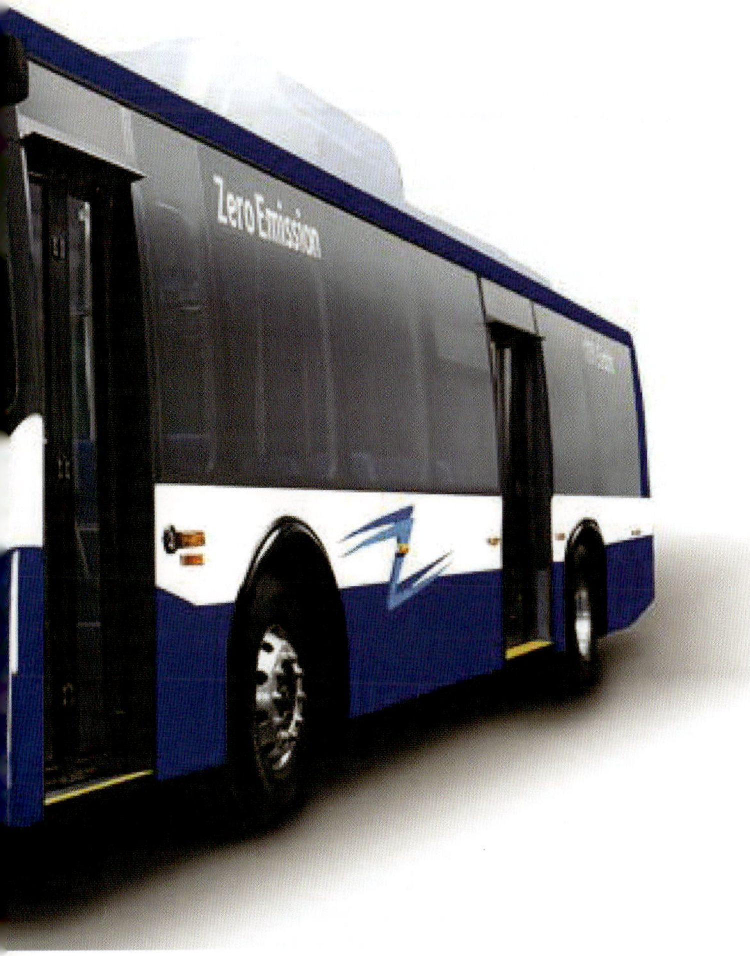

model could be viable and profitable. The bus design should align with the current styling trends and design cues. Unique styling needs to be evolved to signify the electric vehicle technology and it should able to create an aspirational and proud feeling in the users. Lastly, the final solutions should comply with the statutory requirements of bus codes.

Discovering

Abhikalp has acquired the required knowledge base in terms of softer aspects and the hardcore technological aspects of bus design by working with all OEM bus manufacturers for the last 22 years. The first electric bus has been designed by Abhikalp in 1994 for BHEL. However, now the technology has been changed considerably. Abhikalp has taken this exercise as an evolution of bus considering the passenger requirements, buyer requirements, and the manufacturer requirements. This takes care of all the softer aspects as well as technological aspects of the design project.

Designing

Olectra-BYD has done extensive market research, opened several customer clinics pan-India and tested running of BYD Chinese buses. After analysing all the data coming directly from the customers, the exercise came down to designing 12-meter long and 9-meter long buses. What needed now is to come up with the unique aesthetics which would provide the prominent face and road presence to Olectra-BYD in India.

Delivery

After the market-research phase, the decision has been taken to come up with two different designs for 12M and 9M buses which would be the benchmarked for future standard buses and midi-buses. The overall design has been worked out considering the low-cost batch production of buses with all the technological and production processes for local manufacturing.

Way Forward

Both the products have been successful in terms of meeting the target requirements. Today both the products are running in various Indian cities successfully. As it is said that no design is absolute design and changes are the part of the product life cycle. Time has come to upgrade the design after two years to much futuristic level and new variants as per new customer requirements.

Client Speak

Both the buses have been pitted against the benchmark BYD vehicles worldwide and they stood well against them. Customers are happy to receive world-class products at Indian price. Clients are also happy to be the market leader in India in electric buses.

HONDA
The Power of Dreams

Honda X-Blade 160

CONTACT INFORMATION

Company Name: Honda R & D (India) Private Limited

Company Address: Technical Center, Plot no. 02, Sector 03, IMT Manesar, Gurugram, Haryana -122050

Name of Contact Person: Kashyap Josyula

Contact Number: +91 9643919934

Email Address: kashyap.josyula@hrdap.mail.a.rd.honda.co.jp

Website URL: http://world.honda.com

The Problem

The trend of adapting 160 cc segment bikes by urban youngsters had been increasing. Very few options of bikes matching this trendy and stylish character were available. Also it was very important to make motorcycles at an affordable price point.

The Plan

Honda R&D (India) had been actively involved along with HMSI during Delhi Auto-Expos through displaying couple of concept-models originated in India for Indian users.

Displaying concepts at such events gave the design team and planning team, an opportunity to gather structured feedback about the needs and demands of the young generation of India.

The data coming through preliminary surveys in Auto-Expo encouraged and helped the team in setting up a new list of the expected styling themes, features, and engine specs.

Discovering

Post analyzing the demands of the most popular segment (150–160 cc), more focused surveys were planned and executed. Extensive but focused feedback was taken from urban as well as semi-urban areas of India.

Trend study surveys carried out on timely basis is an important tool used by designers to strengthen the concept initiated during designing motorcycle in this segment.

Multiple rounds of discussions with various relevant teams led us to a few concrete directions for product offerings in this range.

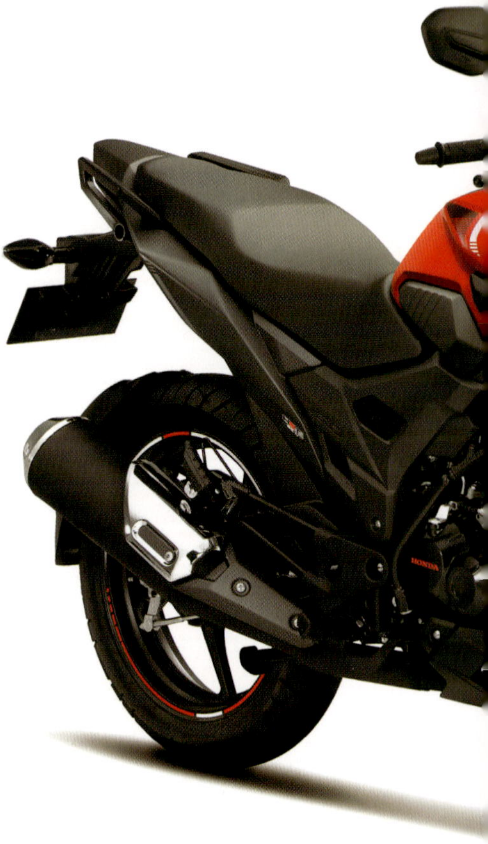

Delivery

After thoughtful analysis of the segment-users by experts, Honda R&D could realize a package which offers best combination of trendy design and affordability. It was a moment where designer could realize the styling and the trend that they had been imagining. Extensive sessions of sketching and many fruitful discussions made way to selection of one final design. Adaptation of modern features such as LED headlight and tail light, all digital meter cutting aero paths and dual exhaust muffler enhanced its appeal manifold. Safety features like ABS and rear disc brake options gave more confidence and assurance to youngsters while riding in the city.

Adaptation of the very popular HET technology helped Honda to move a step closer by manufacturing yet another environment friendly product.

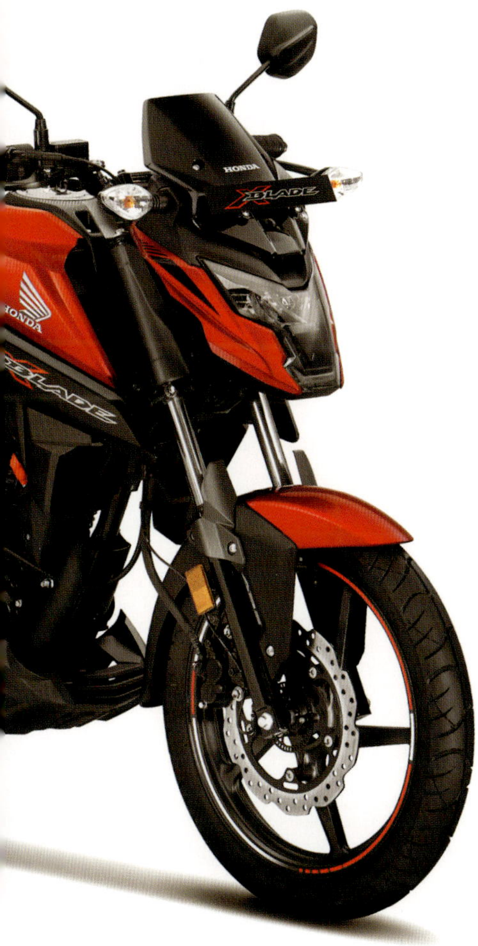

Looking Back

After its launch in February 2018, it has been appreciated by the users as well as the auto journalists across India. It is also being exported to similar markets in other continents.

Steady increase in sales volume observed in the last one year gives a positive indication about the future of this product. Its design offers flexibility and scope for updating it in the future so as to keep appealing the youngsters.

Client Speak

Commenting on the launch, Minoru Kato, President and CEO, Honda Motorcycle and Scooter India Pvt. Ltd: “Strengthening our position in 150-180cc motorcycle segment, the X-Blade defines advanced styling and superior technology for the young enthusiast. We are determined to transform the way India rides on two wheels with new innovative products and advanced technology.”

“The X-Blade has been exclusively designed for the young motorcycle enthusiast looking for style and performance in their daily commuting,” said Yadvinder Singh Guleria, Senior Vice President - Sales and Marketing, Honda Motorcycle and Scooter India Pvt. Ltd.

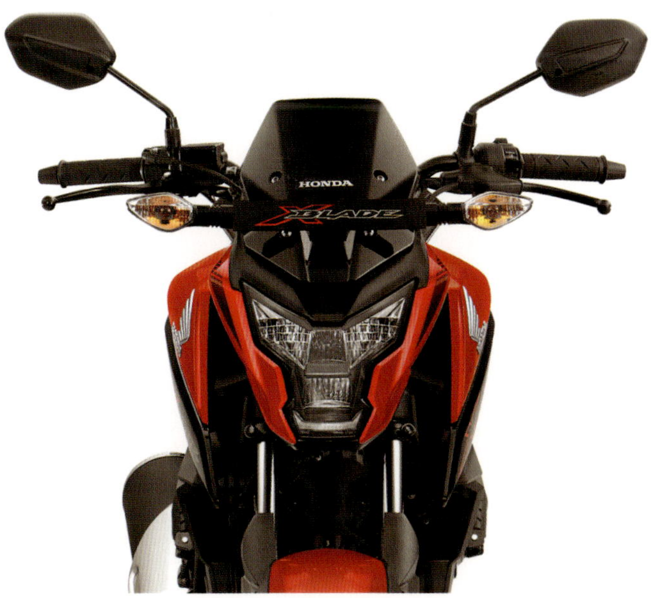

Mahindra
Rise.

Mahindra Furio – Intermediate Commercial Vehicle

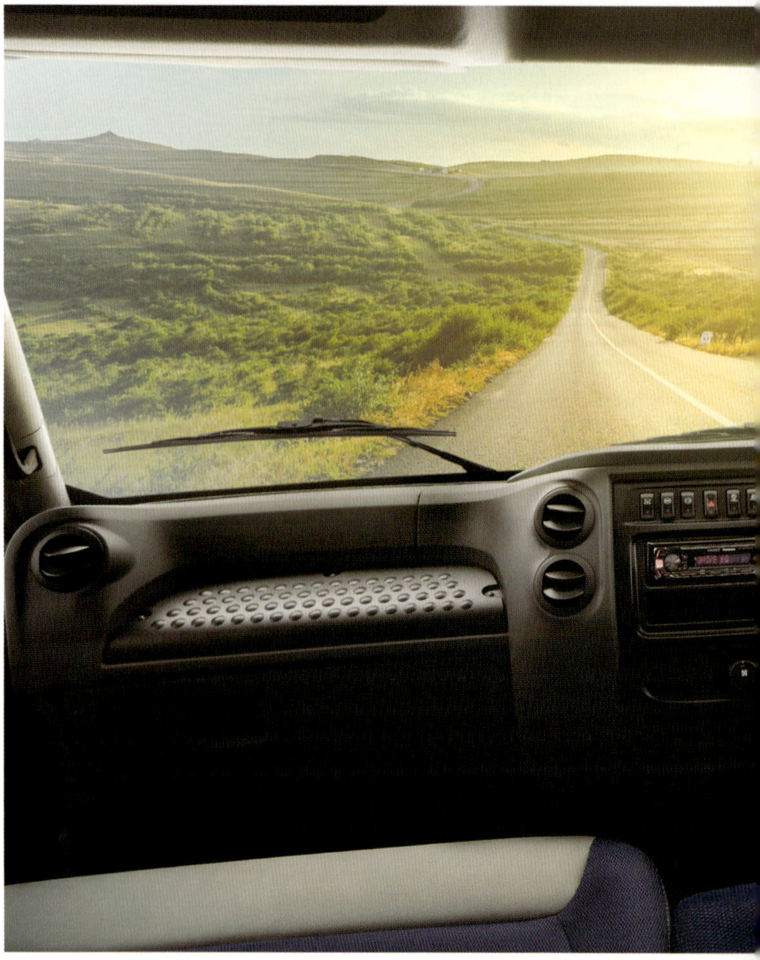

CONTACT INFORMATION

Company Name: Mahindra & Mahindra Ltd

Company Address: Gateway Building, Apollo Sunder, Mumbai 400 001

Name of Contact Person: Ramkripa Ananthan, Principal Chief Designer

Email Address: ANANTHAN.RAMKRIPA@mahindra.com

Website URL: https://www.mahindratruckandbus.com/

The Problem

The Mahindra Furio is Mahindra's entry into the ICV market. It intends to secure Mahindra's place as a full-range commercial vehicle player in the goods segment, with an unprecedented customer value proposition – "Get more profit or give the truck back."

The Plan

Pininfarina and Mahindra put their experiences and skills to better interpret the needs of the ICV segment, with a final goal to design a truck that best expresses the character of the brand.

Designing

For the Furio, Pininfarina developed an exterior style that conveys solidity combined with dynamism. Along with the Mahindra team, Pininfarina defined a truck that integrates aesthetics, function, and innovation. Great attention has been given to its proportions, both in terms of its volumes and graphically.

The design considers the modularity of the vehicle, balancing the form to work well in all its different versions. Focus on interior was crucial. The Furio is designed around the driver and the co-driver, providing for innovative ways to enhance their comfort, productivity and safety. The low rake on the windshield ensures low sun load, resulting in a much cooler cabin, improving occupant comfort in the tropical weather conditions.

Delivery

The Mahindra Furio improves operating economics through its high payload capacity, best-in-class mileage,

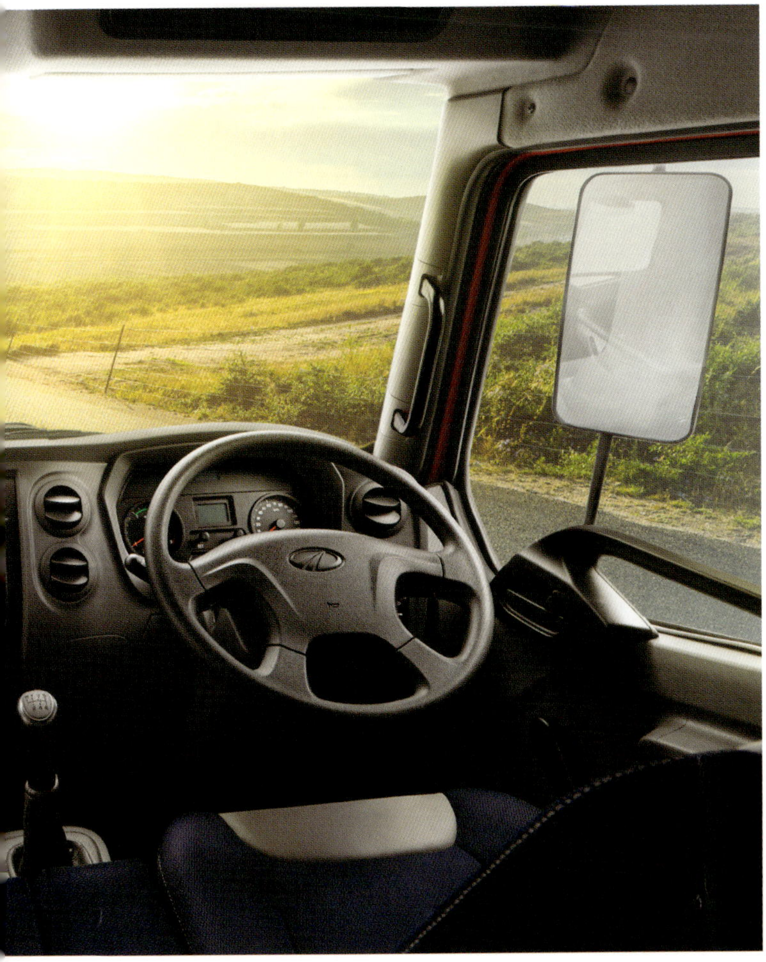

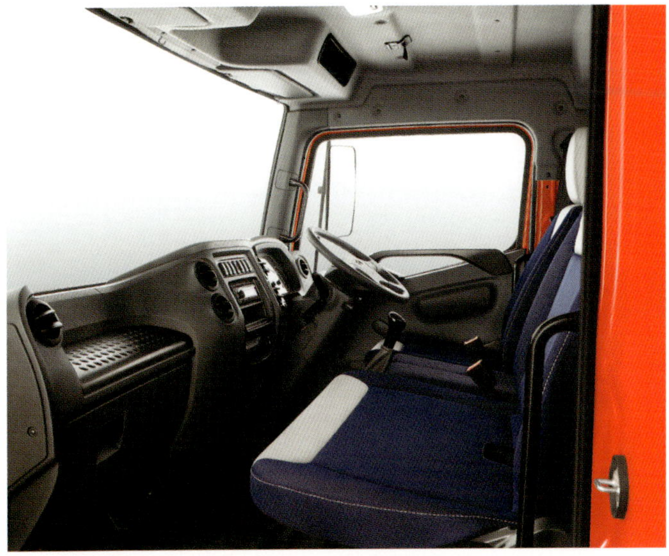

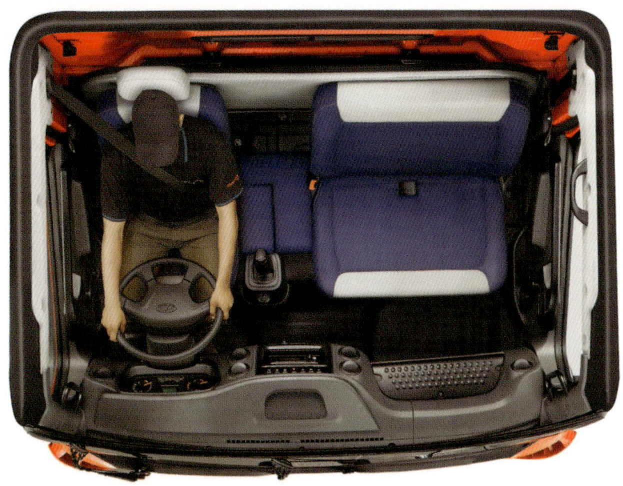

low maintenance costs and better engine power management. Its light-weight engine is equipped with the patented Mahindra FuelSmart technology, optimizing fuel consumption. The FURIO comes with many industry-first and thoughtful features built around the truck driver. The walk-through cabin, flat driver resting seat, provision for seating three persons and intelligent storage space are some of them. The Furio also features a sleeper berth in a day cabin.

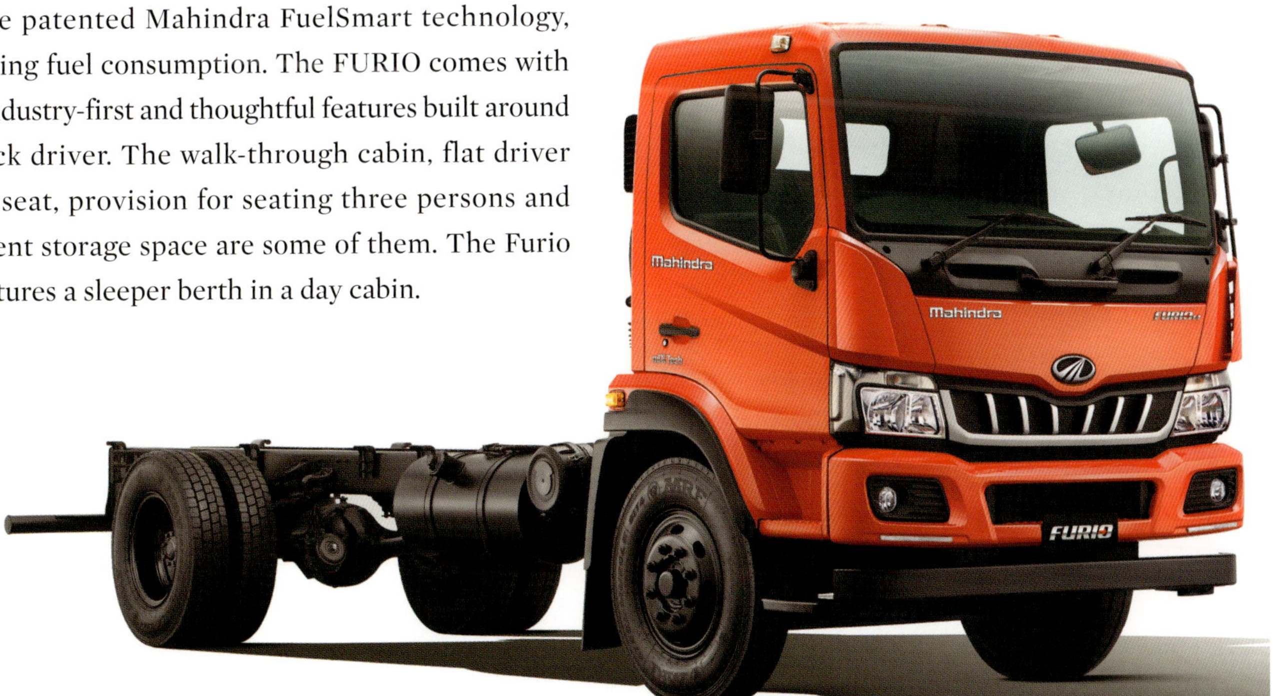

Mahindra
Rise.

Mahindra Marazzo

CONTACT INFORMATION

Company Name: Mahindra & Mahindra Ltd
Company Address: Gateway Building, Apollo Sunder, Mumbai 400 001
Name of Contact Person: Ramkripa Ananthan, Principal Chief Designer
Email Address: ANANTHAN.RAMKRIPA@mahindra.com
Website URL: https://www.mahindratruckandbus.com/

The Problem

Design a '*pa and pals*' car, a car that creates a connect with friends and with family.

The Plan

The Mahindra Design and Pininfarina teams worked to design for a strong brand connect and a strong individual identity.

Discovering

Voice of Customers, captured through user research, gave immense insights to the design team for ideation. The patented body-on-frame, with front-wheel drive (FWD) architecture, and a wide track provided the Marazzo a low and planted stance. The need for easy ingress and egress placed the sill and the H point down. This, coupled with a dead rear axle, enabled a raked-back roof, all without compromising the Mahindra DNA of command seating.

The Turn

With a commitment to creating intrigue by design, the designers at Mahindra took inspiration from nature, along with customer insights. A concept, with its sleek streamlined silhouette, narrowing facia and the aggressive Mahindra grill, was inspired by the movement, shape and expression of a shark. This was shortlisted and further augmented with shark-inspired cues.

Designing

The Mahindra connect is to have the fundamentals of a dominant stance, full bold volumes and taut muscular surfaces. Taking the shark-inspired design cues further, the side profile is sculpted to show agility. The headlamps and taillamps keep true to the theme.

On the interiors, the design cues are unique, robust and contemporary. The design is edgy – a chiselled decorative element and the tech features on the cluster and the infotainment touch screen creates a mood – 'Premium Tech'. The roof liner, with its integrated air distribution system, is an innovative idea. The aircraft throttle inspired parking brake, which adds to the premium feel of the MPV, is a space generating idea.

The colour way (CMF) of a deep shade of blue-black with sharp contrasts, and the in-house developed layered technical grain for the topper areas, emphasize the feeling of space and modernity.

Delivery

The Mahindra Design team worked with North American Technical Centre (MNATC) set up in Detroit, Michigan and the Mahindra Research Valley (MRV), in Chennai to deliver the Marazzo.

A highly experienced team of Studio Engineers helped the designers achieve some of its finer aspects. Its silhouette and surface detailing provide a coefficient of

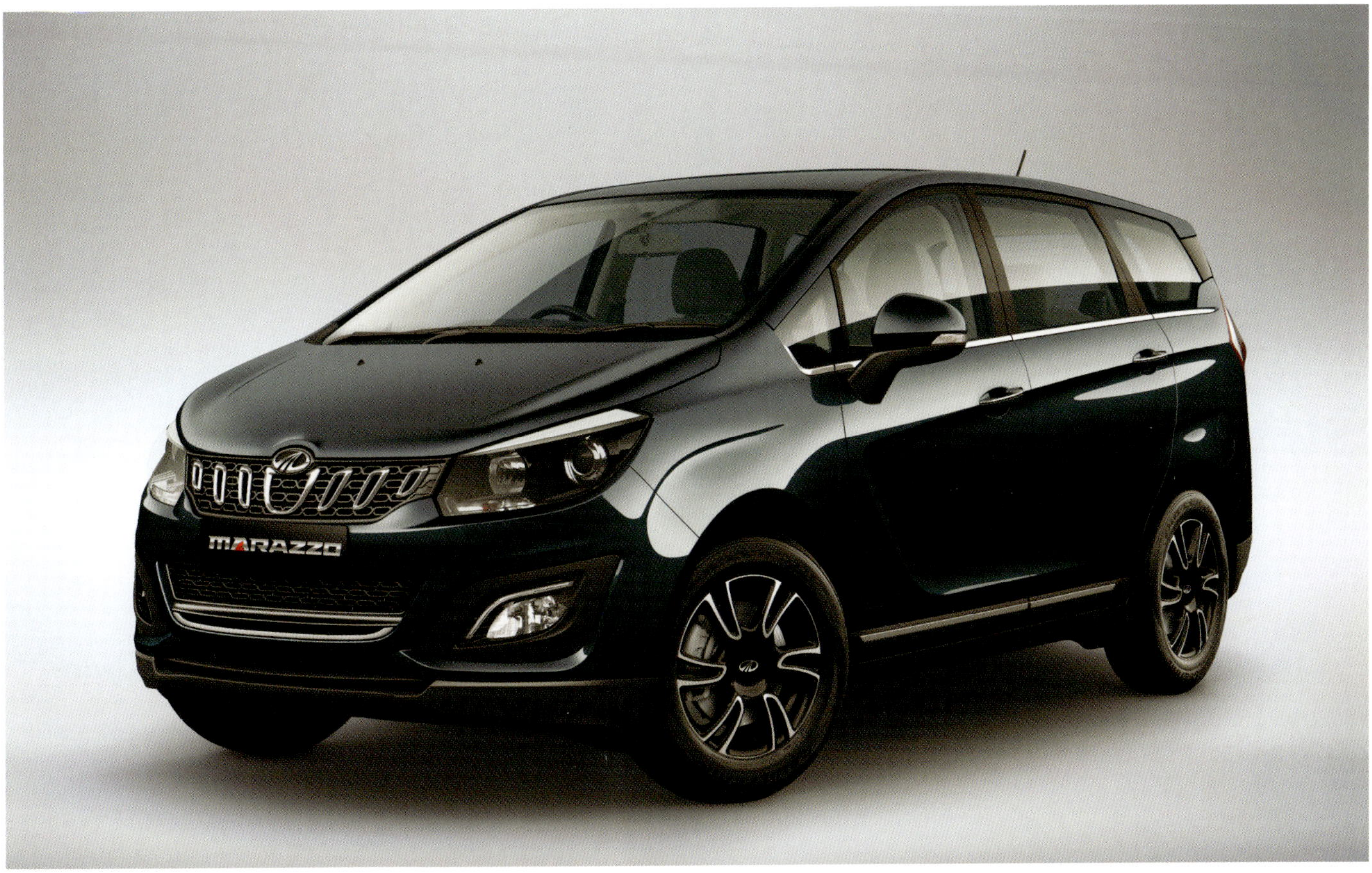

drag of 0.354. The tautly stretched body panels display the Mahindra DNA of robustness with emotive quality. Storage spaces, sensitive, and smart detailing on the interiors achieve a quantum leap in perceived quality.

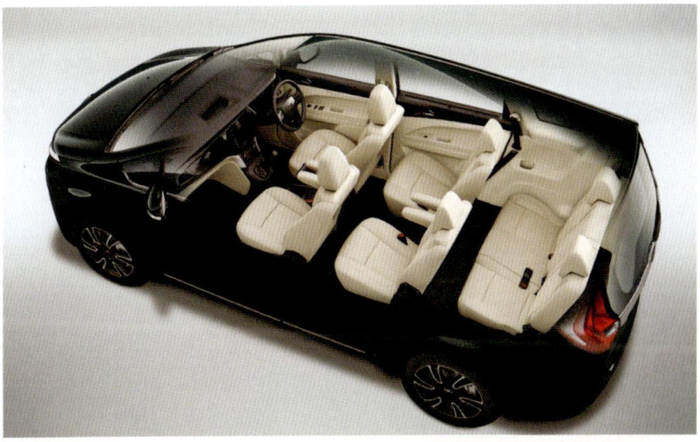

Looking Back

The outcome of this project is not just a methodical conversion of the Voice of Customer (VOC) and the Design Brief, but a passionate and collaborative effort of many dedicated professionals across the globe, a result Mahindra Design are quite proud of.

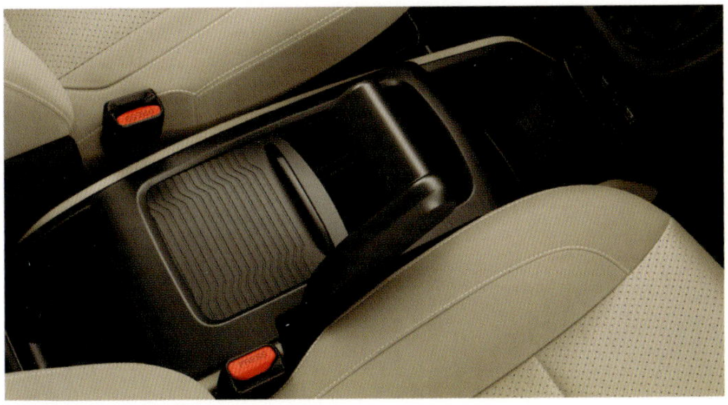

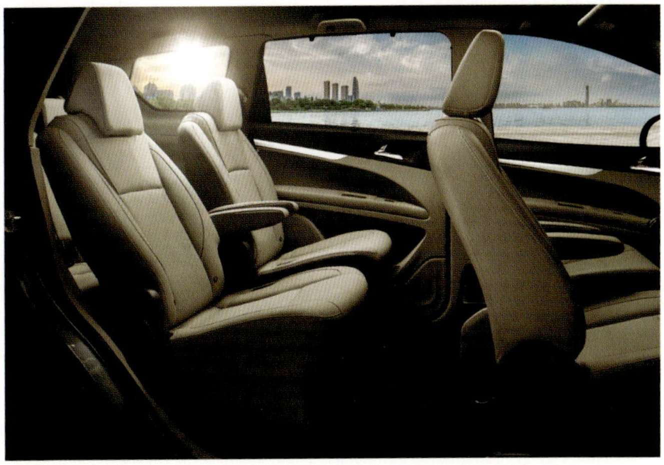

Mahindra XUV300 - The Flamboyant SUV

CONTACT INFORMATION

Company Name: Mahindra & Mahindra Ltd

Company Address: Gateway Building. Apollo Sunder. Mumbai 400 001

Name of Contact Person: Ramkripa Ananthan, Principal Chief Designer

Email Address: ANANTHAN.RAMKRIPA@mahindra.com

Website URL: https://www.mahindratruckandbus.com/

The Problem

Design a flamboyant compact SUV to meet the customers' latent desire for power and pizzazz, that best expresses Mahindra's design language.

The Plan

The compact SUV segment is a very competitive one. Mahindra collaborated with its sister concern, SsangYong Motor, who already had a similar vehicle in their portfolio. The SsangYong Tivoli is distinguished by a youthful look and a robust platform. The brief for the XUV300 was to leverage the lineage of the XUV500 on that platform.

Designing

Designers from the India and Korea design studios shaped this cheetah cub together. The optimal volume of the SsangYong platform was modified for the Indian market needs for sub 4M length, high ground clearance, short overhangs and the formal requirements that reflect Mahindra design. This collaboration also led to

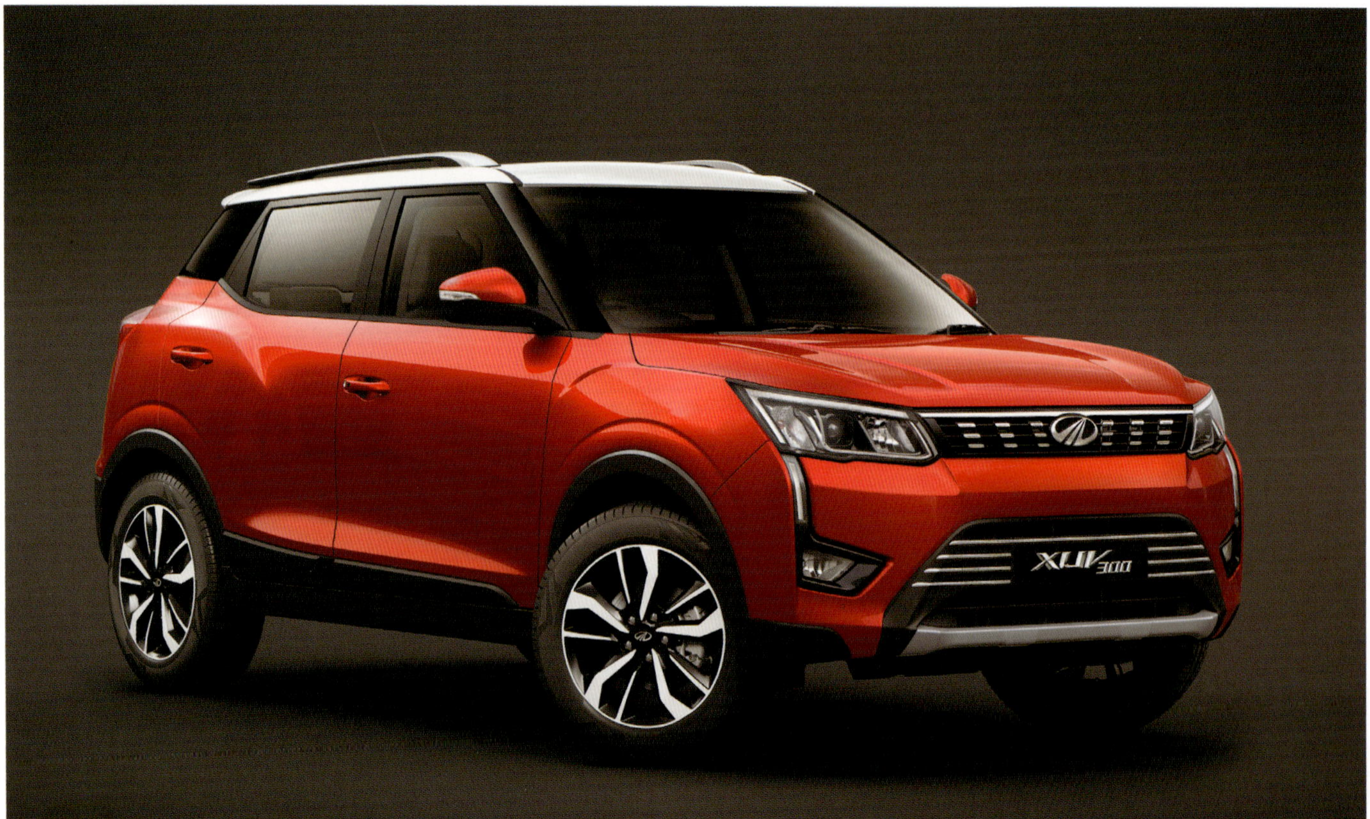

a reciprocal influence and design language convergence which reflects the fact that the differences between Indian and International tastes are reducing more and more.

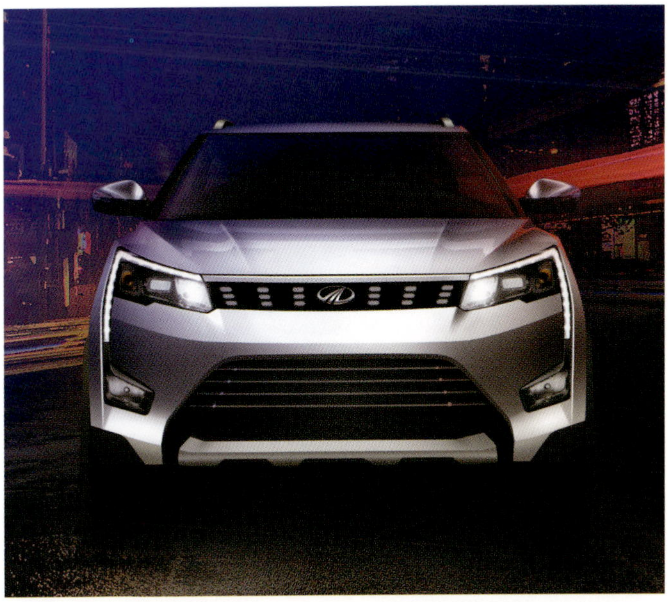

Delivery

With its aggressive front grille, chiseled body and imposing stance, the XUV300 always looks ready to charge. Its projector headlamps and striking LED Daytime Running Lamps leave a lasting impression. While its unique LED tail lamps create an indelible visual signature. Add to this the sporty, 17" Diamond Cut Alloys, and you have an SUV that meets every demand of the urban jungle, in style.

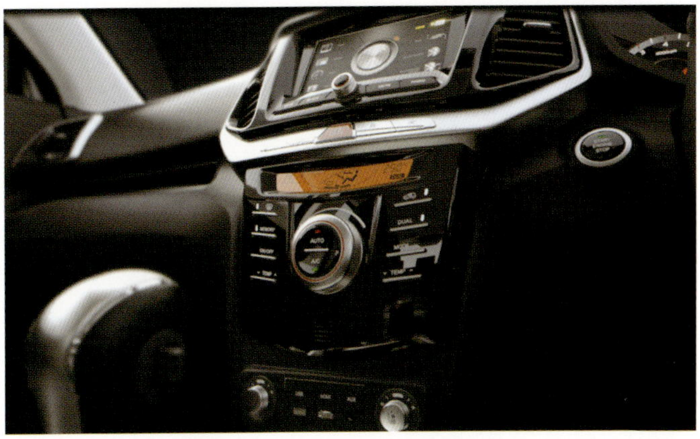

Its spacious cabin, finely crafted, dual-tone dashboard and a sophisticated, electric sunroof elevate the standard of luxury to new heights. Premium leatherette seats with well-designed bolsters and a leather-wrapped steering wheel add to the focus on perceived quality.

Looking Back

The Indian market is very challenging. The XUV300 sets a new benchmark for design and quality for Mahindra.

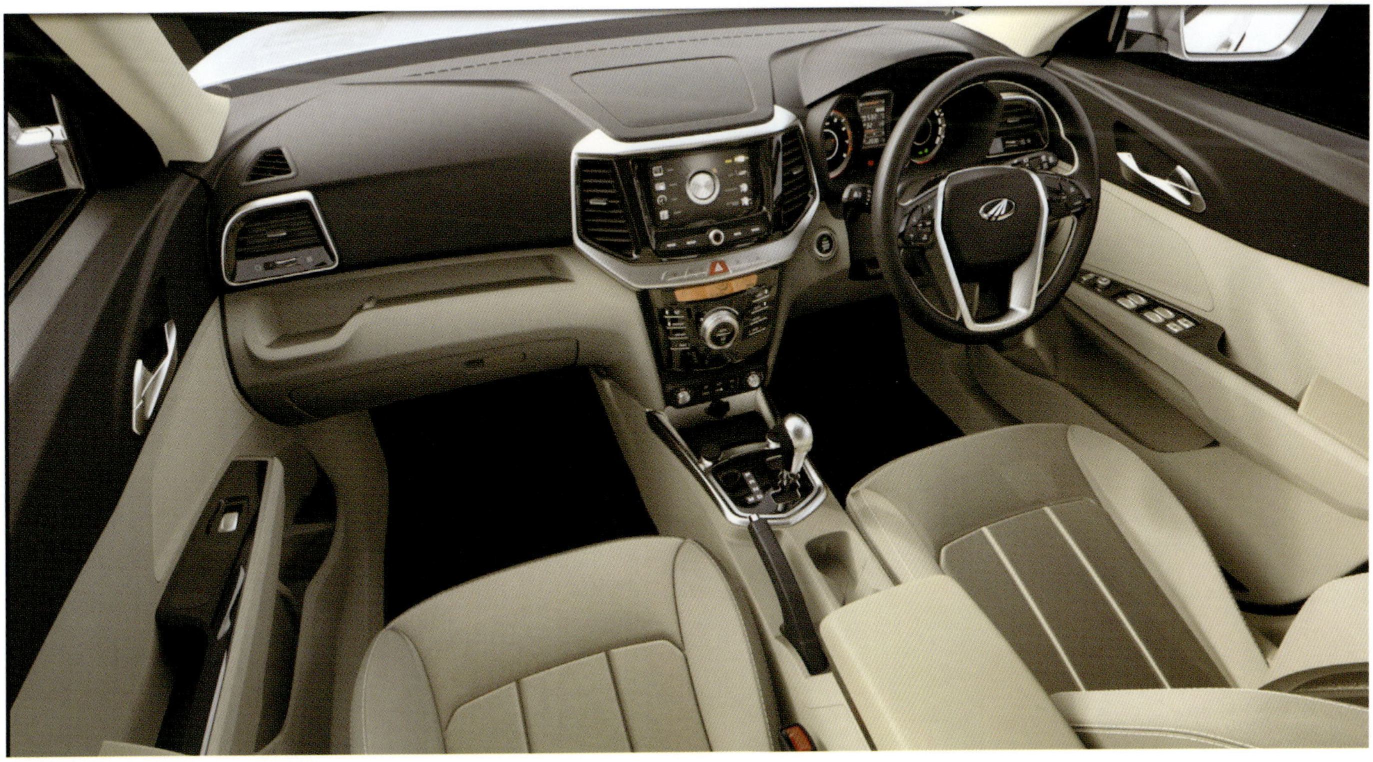

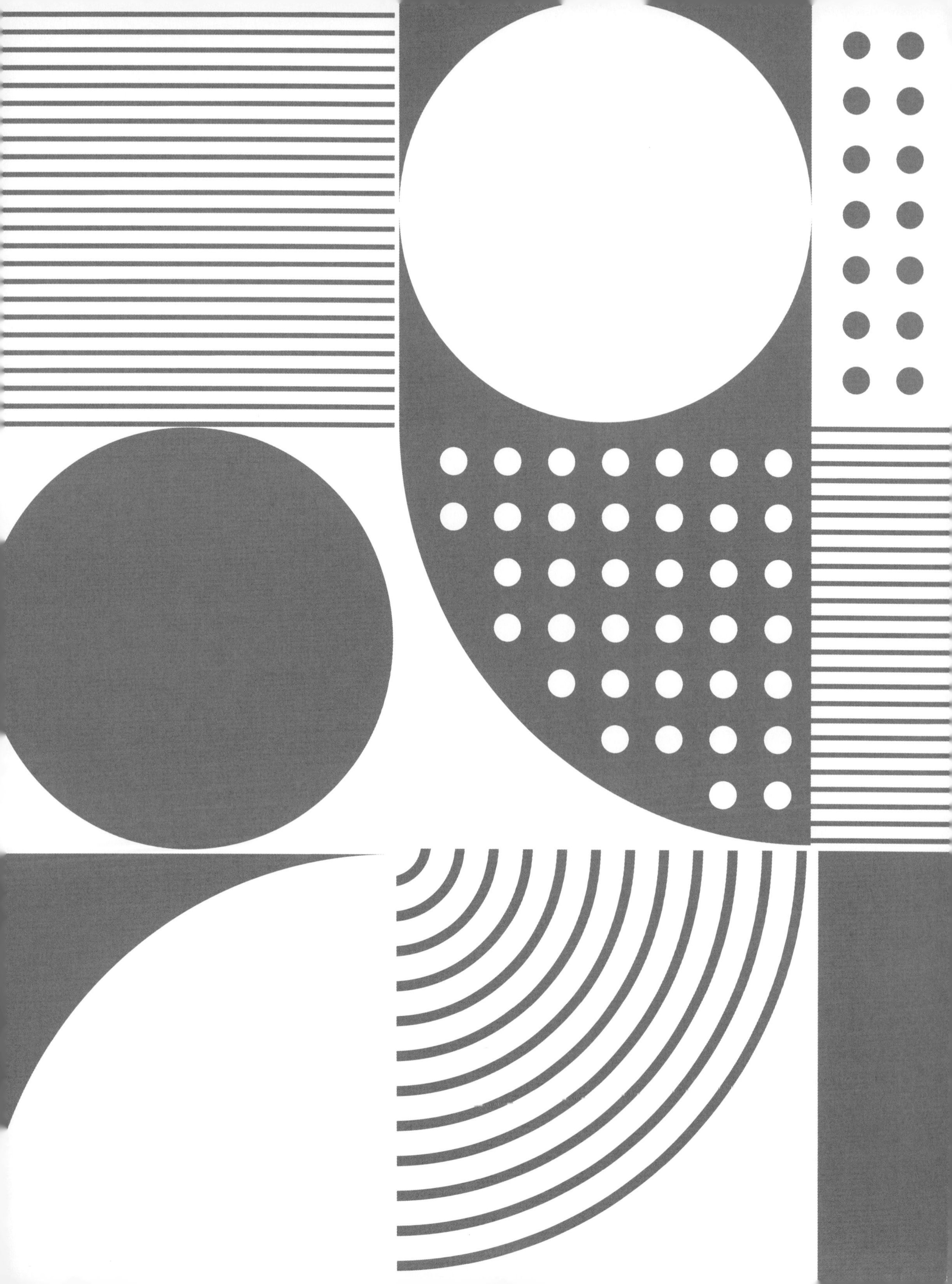

POSITION PAPER

Traditional Crafts

Employment and Entrepreneurship Opportunities in Traditional Crafts

Dr. Toolika Gupta, Director,
Indian Institute of Craft and Design

Preamble

Handcrafted products have carved a niche for themselves worldwide in this era of mass production. In India however, there are multiple dimensions when we talk of the craft sector. It is evident from many schemes of the government and by the immense efforts invested by the NGOs that Indians including NRIs understand the value and want to revive our traditional but languishing crafts. We also want our crafts to be appreciated and recognized all over the world. There are many crafts that have been revived to healthy levels by the efforts of the people dedicated to the cause. Largely, these have been NGOs like Sewa and Dastkar, which have helped the revival of crafts that have generated employment. As we progress further, we need to empower the craftsmen by teaching them design and entrepreneurship, which will encourage the next generation to be inducted into the traditional craft practices.

In this paper it is proposed that rather than only looking at employment opportunities, we need to impart design and entrepreneurial skills to the artisans to make them more competitive and successful in the economic terms. These crafts need to be looked at as great businesses as they were once upon a time. To increase employment in the traditional craft sector, an angle of craft tourism, developing exclusive high-quality products and branding of regional crafts are required. If the craftsmen and women get decent incomes and the respect that they deserve, coupled with use of modern technology to aid them, our crafts will not perish, which seems inevitable in today's time. This will encourage the young children of craftsmen to pursue their own trade and will be a boon for the society.

Introduction

According to UNESCO and ITC (International Trade Centre), *Final Report of the International Symposium on Crafts and the International Market: Trade and Customs Codification, 1997*, the definition of craft is as follow:

Products that are produced by artisan, either completely by hand or with the help of hand-tools or even mechanical means, as long as the direct contribution of the artisan remains the most substantial component of the finished product. The special nature of the artisan products derives from their distinctive features, which can be utilitarian, aesthetic, artistic, creative, culturally attached, decorative, functional, traditional, religiously and socially symbolic and significant. (UNESCO, n.d.)

The traditional crafts of our country can be divided into hard goods and soft goods. The hard goods comprise the products made of materials such as wood, metal, stone, or even with clay and baked like pottery, ceramics, glass and similar kind of products. The soft material goods comprise of textiles, clothes in general, leather, paper products and products made from grass, reeds or similar type of fibres. According to the Ministry of Textiles (Development Commisioner (Handicrafts), 2019) the handicraft industry provides employment to 7 million artisans (including those in carpet trades), which include a large number of women and people belonging to the economically weaker section of the society.

The handicraft sector has a high potential for employment and requires lower levels of investment.

India is one of the leading suppliers of handicrafts in the world market. Manika Dhama writes that "The handicraft and handloom sector in India is a ₹24,300-crore industry and contributes nearly ₹10,000 crore annually in the export earnings. The 12th Five Year Plan had projected that it would become the largest non-farm sector in rural India, swelling its workforce by 10 per cent, doubling the output and exporting 18 per cent more during 2012-17." She discusses the problems faced by the industry including infrastructure, poor market, tough competition by mass produced goods (Dhama, 2015). The article discusses a lot of issues and brings to light the role of government and private NGOs in the sector.

An initiative that was taken up by Padma Shri awardee Ms Laila Tayabji in the form of Dastkar was to generate employment in the craft sector, similarly many other big and small NGOs and educational institutes such as Kala Raksha, Judy Frater's Somaya Kala Vidyalaya and Sally Holkar's The Handloom School were all targeted towards the growth in the hand-crafted textiles. The National Institute of Design and The National Institute of Fashion Technology have both given a boost to this sector. The focus has been on handlooms, as textiles and that too hand-woven textiles have had a major share in the economy.

Many government schemes such as USTAAD and SAMARTH, and government agencies such as KVIC, EPCH (Export Promotion Council of Handicrafts) have all focussed on Indian handicrafts as it is a sector that makes unique Indian textiles. The last Handloom Census of India 2009-10, conducted by National Council of Applied Economic Research (NCAER) and sponsored by the Development Commissioner (Handlooms), Ministry of Textiles, Government of India was the third National Handloom Census of weavers and allied workers. This states that the distribution of adult (18 years and above) handloom workers by employment status: independent workers in rural area–2,173,343, in urban area–178,279. Those under master weavers/private owners in rural areas are 907,855 and in urban areas are 391,146. Those under some institutions were 151,027 in rural area and 45,185 in the urban area (National Council of Applied Economic Research, 2010).

The second census was conducted in 1995, and when compared with the 2010 census, one can see that the number of handloom-weaver households has gone down by almost 3 lakhs. The handloom weaver count has almost gone down by 5 lakhs, now these figures are not very encouraging. We do not have much idea of the handicraft census, though we can see a list of the artisans on the website of the Development Commissioner of Handlooms. Mohanty writes about the craft artisans in the urban informal sector and details well the juxtaposition of the formal and the informal sector (Mohanty, 2009). He focuses on the silver smiths in Orissa, who carry out the filigree work. He writes about how the work is really valued, but when it comes to artisans, the number is really small. Keshab Das emphasizes on this and points out that the labour of the craftsmen is undervalued, and rightly states that even many years after Independence, and after many schemes by the government, nothing much has really been done for this unorganized sector (Das, 2017)

Brinda Viswanathan's *Enumeration of Crafts Persons in India* published in 2013 by Madras School of economics has a lot of data on various crafts of the country (Viswanathan, 2013).

Craft and Design Education

The issue of education in this sector is addressed by the Indian Institute of Crafts and Design. As the Director of the Institute, I would like to emphasize the vision of the institute which is 'to continue to invigorate the craft sector and to become the centre of excellence in Crafts and Design, encouraging research and bringing new life to the languishing crafts of India.' The students, who graduate from the institute have a keen understanding in this sector and are also taught entrepreneurial skills. IICD was also a partner in 2017 for the program which was known as 'Crafting Luxury and Lifestyle Businesses' launched by IIM Ahmedabad. IICD was also a partner in 2018 with Craft Accelerator launched by the start-up Oasis. Both these programs were targeted towards entrepreneurship in the craft sector.

Many other institutes in the country, including design institutes, engineering, agriculture, marketing and many faculties devoted to research and design should provide appropriate interventions, and reasons for employment in this sector. The craft sector has been one of the oldest in the country, it is common knowledge today that Indian handicrafts were being exported from India since the days of the Indus Valley civilization. Unfortunately, we have not addressed this very important sector in the modern education at school or college level. It is merely reduced to a hobby due to the colonial mindset and is not seen as a potential source of future employment.

The British set up art institutes and referred to the crafts in India as 'Industrial Arts'. These schools that were set up in India, like the one in Jaipur, finally became only art institutes, promoting art but not craft. Due to industrialization, cheap and mass-produced goods were easily available. India realized the need of engineering schools and later of a design school. Our design school, NID (National Institute of Design) was modelled on Bauhaus and became a hub of industrial design. Sadly, the crafts were left behind.

Entrepreneurship in Crafts

In 1995, the Government of Rajasthan along with the stalwarts from NID, decided to launch an institute of crafts. This was a wonderful vision for India's future. The institute was set up to foster creativity in the craft sector and to create 'design-techno-managers'. We have now come a long way from the last 25 years and IICD or the Indian Institute of Crafts and Design, has paved way for the future leaders and entrepreneurs in the craft sector. The skill of hand-crafting, with the right amount of mechanical and technical intervention, coupled with design thinking, gives result to excellent products that are based on the requirement of the user. The thought that this excellent product should be able to tell a story of its own, and the crafts person should be able to take it to its customers, has paved the way for craft entrepreneurs.

While it is important to be gainfully employed, it is more important to be able to offer gainful employment to many. With emphasis on entrepreneurship in the craft sector, I believe, we will be able to create wealth of the people of the country, not only in terms of money and product, but also in terms of sustainable goals that have been set up by the United Nations. With our focus on the entrepreneurship in the craft sector, we are certain to meet the United Nations' Sustainable Development Goals focusing on poverty alleviation, sustainable livelihoods and eco-friendly living.

'Design Diligence'

Need for a new attitude in the practice of Design in India

Ms. Darshan Gandhi, Global Head - Design,
Godrej Consumer Products Limited

The clutter due to mass production is evident in the marketplaces and in our minds as we are constantly consuming *more* of everything; be it tangible or digital. The constant need to create newness and scope of finding sweet spots of meaningful differentiations is getting narrower as we all evolve. This demands for redefining the 'role of design' as a function in each sector, where it needs to play a critical role toward decluttering, redefining and reimagining the content. What it simply means that we need to move the needle from theoretical idea of design to pragmatic idea of design. The age of abundance calls for mental calisthenics.

"Once we over-learn something, we cease to know it anymore at all"

"The age of abundance is over, I remember thinking, not because things are no longer abundant, but because abundance has lost its status as our reigning aspiration."
– Young Me Moon in *Different*

With the current model of design practices, we are only making incremental changes. The role of design is mainly centred around creating products, brands or experiences.

This is specifically in context of the way design as a discipline has been positioned in the Indian industries that require a twofold shift as follows:

1. Design education and attitude shift in a designer's own role.

Prepping up designers to be ready to deal with greater complexity of human interactions, people management, interdisciplinary working, leadership skills, project management, communication and decision making is becoming critical for a designer to succeed and practice design in any sector. The design tools themselves are not good enough, thus enabling designers to create joyous environments and meaningful conversations in the workplace before creation calls for a critical reflection in the design curriculum.

2. Recruiting relevant design disciplines for your sector is a first right step and the most critical one of all.

The industries need to know the discipline of design through case-studies, success stories to be able to position and place relevant design streams in their respective industries in a manner that it does not remain an esoteric or a siloed but truly a pragmatic approach. We need the facilitators, who can fill in this gap and create awareness about good design practices in the need of the time. The report on 'The Business Value of Design' by McKinsey Design that gives a holistic view on full potential of design leading to change provides good insights - https://www.mckinsey.com/business-functions/mckinsey-design/our-insights/the-business-value-of-design

The utopian view on 'Design'

Good Design = Good Business
Design = Human centric approach
Design + Detail = Delight
Design = Differentiation
Design = Connecting dots
Design = System design
Design = Change
Design = Happiness
Design = Empathy

Design = Premiumisation

Design = Value for money

Good Design = Apple

Design = Sustainability

While in an ideal world these are all the possible outcomes of a good design practice, it remains theoretical or aspirational in our context until we adapt it indigenously. A lot of these have been practiced in the western world and they have fully realised the value of good design practice with greater understanding of the subject.

The bigger questions that remain for Design in India are — 'Are our industries ready to optimize the best practices of design?' Or 'do the designers know what role they have to play in changing the mindset around their work environments directly impacting the outcome?'

There exists a massive gap and thus a humongous opportunity for the Indian industries to inculcate good design practices. While changing the world could be a tall order, if used with right model, design can indeed make a pleasant difference in the way one can look at opportunity and definitely create more dynamic organisations.

Below are some of the observations and learnings as thought starters for the design boom in India.

An Indigenous view on 'Design'

Design = Disciplines

There are several design disciplines and the needs of each sector calls for the relevant disciplines applicable in their context. Often two or more disciplines need to work together to cater to a specific problem. This requires attention both by the design institutions during placement as well as by the design managers. This also includes the consideration of complementary creative disciplines which often is substituted as design discipline.

Design = Operating Model

One cannot copy-paste design models from Google, Apple or PepsiCo. Creating an environment for design to strive and thrive in the industry itself is an exercise of one's own vision.

The model has to be cultivated, iterated and be constantly evolving. We need design promoters to take an active role in understanding this tool before adapting into it. We also need design managers who are fully aware and well equipped in influencing the leadership.

Design = Integration

Good design has a part serving and a part visioning function; design being developed in-house or outsourced should be inducted in the networks of the industry's systems, values, knowledge and their typical functions to prevent subjective or superficial design outcome. Design needs to function like a floating bubble that can borrow from knowledge networks, insights and attaches itself to various internal/external factors, departments and disciplines to be able to contextualise the opportunities. There is a growing need for designers to design interactions before arriving at the solutions.

Design = Openness

We need to be open to learn from other successful design practices from other developed nations and industries. We need to do our own design research and define our own way of *Indian Design*. A country like India with such deep roots of craft, material sciences, art and cultures we can only enrich the very discipline of design globally!

Design = Economy

Design is a method, a tool to bring order to chaos, to contextualize, to maximize, to re-centre relevance. It's not merely a form factor enhancing tool. We need to normalize this as any other ordinary function within the sectors to evolve both the school of design and the outcome. It can no longer remain an exclusive discipline. Generalization of the design practice can bring greater economies of scale.

Design = Ministry

Design can truly be a strategic advantage for the nation. I would encourage every industry and sector to have a small or big a relevant design presence including government sectors.

We need many more design savvy companies, sectors, cities, experiences. With the government's invested interest, concerted efforts should be directed for the 'Design in India' mission and have our share in global design footprint. The CII Design mission was a great start.

To conclude, design has a dual role to play – One for 'sustenance' and the other as a 'futurist'. The key is in choosing the right balance of both for a true design leadership.

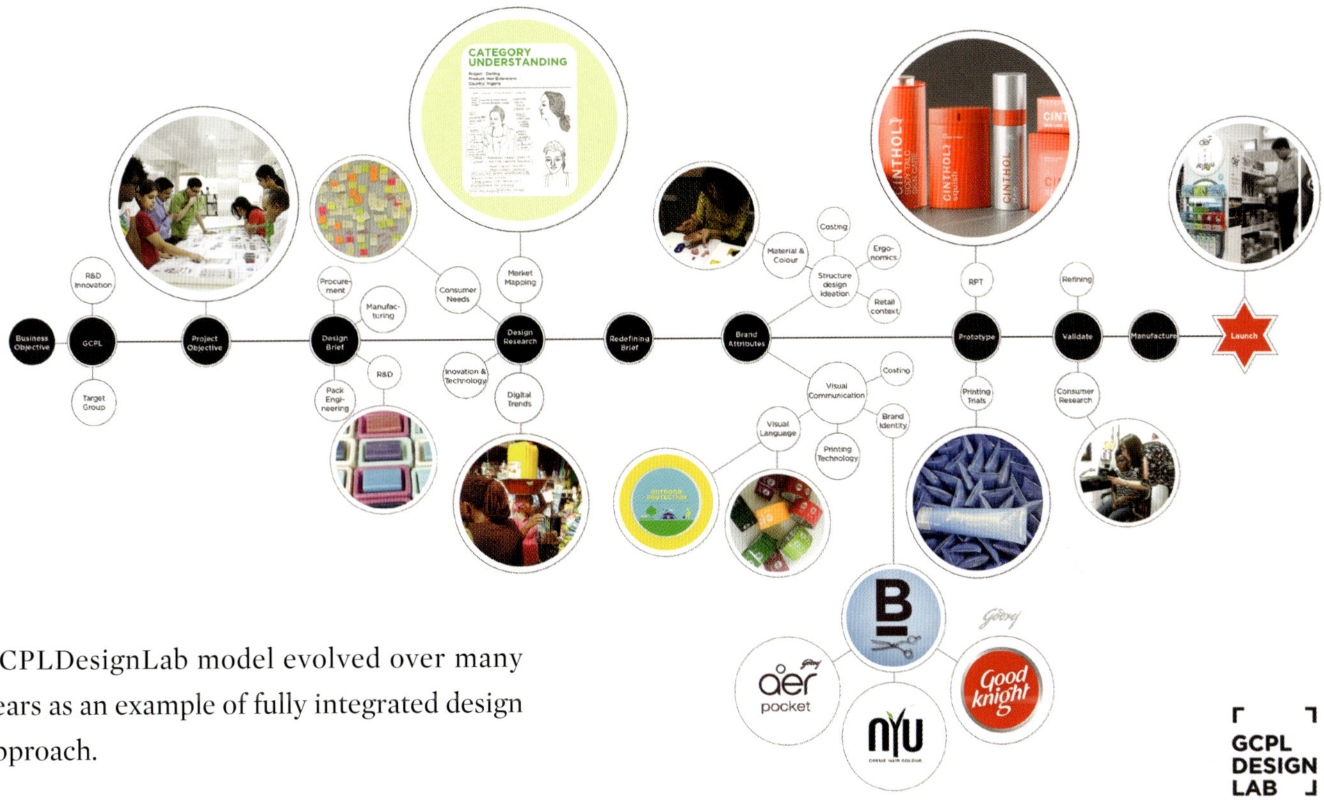

GCPLDesignLab model evolved over many years as an example of fully integrated design approach.

GCPL DESIGN LAB

Design Intervention in Smart Cities

Mr. Vijay Atmakuri, Head of Experience Design, Siemens India

Preamble

Currently, as there is no single official or universally accepted definition of the Smart City, let us look at the Smart Sustainable City definition coming from the United Nations Economic Commission for Europe (UNECE) and International Telecommunication Union (ITU). This definition has been conceptualized after evaluating more than 100 descriptions of Smart City across the globe. It is also in line with the United Nations' Sustainable Development Goal #11, "Make cities and human settlements inclusive, safe, resilient and sustainable," which is:

A smart sustainable city is an innovative city that uses ICTs and other means to improve quality of life, the efficiency of urban operation and services and competitiveness while ensuring that it meets the needs of present and future generations concerning economic, social, and environmental aspects.

1.1 Global Picture

The global population is on the move toward urbanization. According to the United Nations, more than two thirds of the world's citizens will live in cities by 2050, with 90 percent of this urban growth taking place in Asia and Africa.[1]

Given this massive migration to urban areas, the subject of sustainability for cities has been at top of the agenda for many. And rightly so. Governments, municipalities, non-governmental organizations (NGOs), corporations, and global leaders worldwide are all involved and grappling with a fundamental issue: How can the mega-cities of tomorrow provide essential services such as clean water and adequate waste removal? And how can they create transportation infrastructure that reduces the emission of pollutants into the air while accommodating so many.

Today, for instance, some 663 million people around the world do not have access to safe and reliable drinking water.[2] A mass influx of new residents into the world's largest cities will bring a surging tide of issues surrounding access to fresh water for human consumption and basic sanitation.

Mega-cities also throw up "mega" waste disposal issues. The world's cities already generate over 2 billion metric tons of solid waste each year.[3] By 2050, annual waste generation will increase by another 70 percent.[4]

And then there are air quality issues, one of the critical challenges being carbon dioxide (CO^2) emissions. As population epicenters, cities consume over two-thirds of the world's energy and account for more than 70 percent of global CO^2 emissions.[5] This number will only grow as the escalating urban populations demand and use more energy for heating, cooling, and transportation. Smart buildings are vital for overcoming many of these challenges because they are responsible for 36 percent of global energy consumption and nearly 40 percent of direct and indirect CO^2 emissions.[6]

1. United Nations (June 2019), World Population Prospects 2019: Highlights
2. Thirst Project
3. The World Bank (2016), What a Waste 2.0: A Global Snapshot of Solid Waste Management to 2050
4. The World Bank (2019), Solid Waste Management
5. C40 Cities
6. The International Energy Agency, IEA Efficient World Strategy

1.2 Indian Context

The Smart Cities Mission is the Government of India programme launched in 2015 with an ambition to transform 100 cities in India.

The purpose of the Smart Cities Mission is to drive economic growth and improve the quality of life of people by enabling local area development and harnessing technology, especially technology that leads to smart outcomes. Area-based development will transform the existing locations (retrofit and redevelop), including slums, into better-planned ones, thereby improving the liveability of the whole city. New areas (greenfield) will be developed around cities to accommodate the expanding population in urban areas. Application of smart solutions will enable cities to use technology, information, and data to improve infrastructure and services. Overall development in this way will improve quality of life, create employment, and enhance incomes for all, especially the poor and the disadvantaged, leading to inclusive cities.

The implementation of the Mission at the city level will be done by a Special Purpose Vehicle (SPV) created for the purpose. The SPV will plan, appraise, approve, release funds, implement, manage, operate, monitor, and evaluate the Smart City development projects.

Smart Cities Mission guidelines stipulate two strategic components for smart city development: area-based development and pan-city development initiatives.

The area-based development primarily covers three aspects:

- Retrofitting – city improvement
- Redevelopment – city renewal
- Greenfield – city extension

While pan-city development initiatives include the application of the selected smart solution(s) to the existing city-wide infrastructure, after due consultation with citizens, a priority sector will be identified for implementation. The application of intelligent solutions will involve the use of technology, information, and data to make infrastructure and services better.

2.0 Current Scenario

Today's cities have various challenges; some of them are listed below. These challenges not only look massive, but they also pose multiple and tricky questions, like:

- What solves thee challenges?
- What is the best mode of tackling these them?
- Who is the best entity to deal with them?
- Who has the right solution in addressing them?
- Who is responsible for the sustenance of deployed solutions?

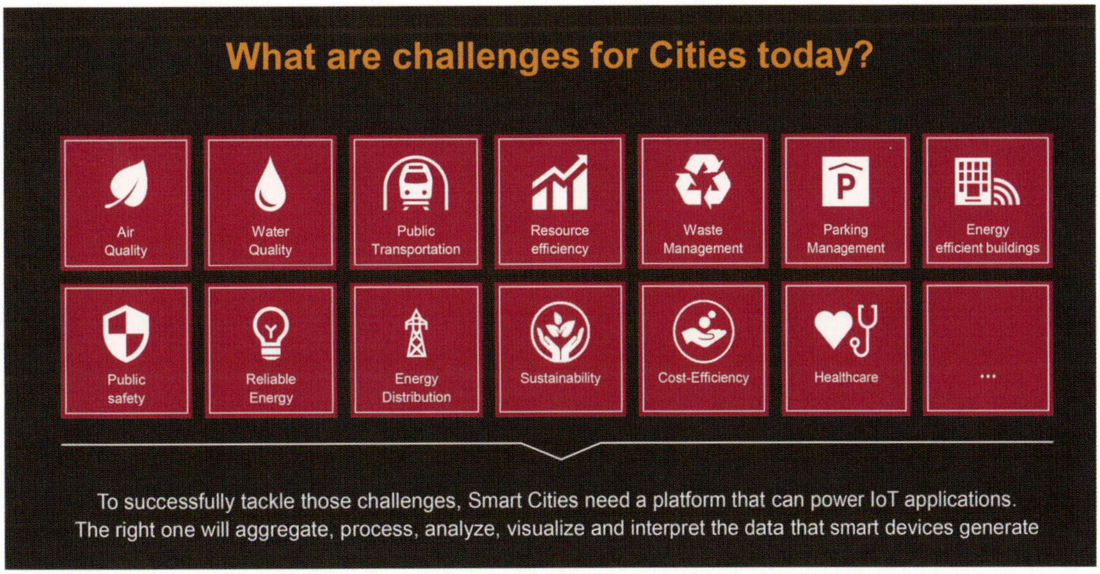

As there is no single solution that can solve any of these challenges, the design team can collaborate with other stakeholders in figuring out the right solution that can be the right fit for the purpose that can ideally leverage the benefit of technologies.

Cities are changing due to new challenges emerging because of the needs of society and even because of the opportunities offered by technologies and modern instruments as in the emerging paradigm of the IoT. The awareness of social and environmental issues forced local and supranational institutions to act.

From a technology and citizen's involvement perspective, as shown in the below figure, at a very high level, cities are classified into three:

- Digital City
- Smart City
- Sustainable Smart City

Digital City, the primary focus is Technology and Innovation, where the realization of technologies is done through a set of modern deployable tools. Here, the primary goals are to digitize a system (or collection of systems) to increase the effectiveness, productivity, or ease.

Smart City, the first change, is in terms of Technology and Services involving a difference in the human aspect as well. It is achieved through the social participation of the citizens. Here, guidelines on how to meet changes in services based on innovative approaches are mainly set, and effectiveness is measured on the scale of making them.

Sustainable Smart City is a new approach to services offered involving the human side of changes towards a sustainable and greener future. Here the goals and KPIs are the primary focus, and the achievement of these goals is significant on a long-time horizon.

The main feature characterizing the digital city is the role of Information and Communications Technology (ICT), considered a necessary tool to improve citizens' quality of life. The smart city thinks the role of new technologies but focuses on citizens' roles as passive actors and active co-creators because they can contribute to the city's governance. Moreover, elements related to sustainability emerge but are intended mainly to keep, for the long term, the results obtained through the smartization process. Finally, concerning the sustainable smart city, as in the previous cases, many elements characterizing the first two conceptions described are recalled but are done so using a new approach and through the filter of modern philosophy: an equitable and balanced set of goals in line with the principles of sustainable development.

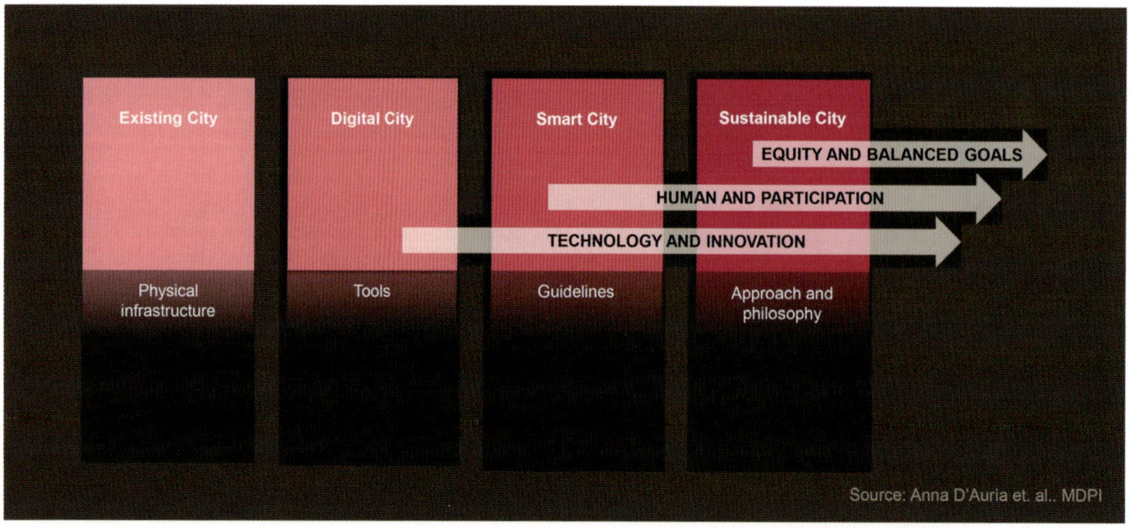

Putting all together, a Smart City is a System of Systems of Systems, encapsulating various in an eco-systems.

3.0 Need for Design Interventions in Smart Cities

At the highest level, the designer has a unique and indispensable role and responsibility in crafting a smart city. Designers work with various stakeholders in understanding and coming up with the right designs and workflows that suite the local and context-sensitive needs that adhere to cultural requirements. The key stakeholders include policymakers, urban planners, standardization bodies, regulatory authorities, governing bodies, public and private enterprises and industrial players who primarily provide technological solutions to that should meet the citizens needs in making a city smart and sustainable.

Designers and design teams work with official bodies in co-creation and collaboration mode primarily to understand their requirements and their planned key performance indicators (KPIs) for the desired Smart City.

Designers work with the consumers of the Smart City, the citizens, to understand their wants, needs, and desires. Here the designers co-create with the citizens to fish out the most significant needs that matter them the most.

By taking all these into account, the design teams come up with the most effective designs for the smart city that meet the official bodies' KPI requirements and at the same time, delivers best-in-class experiences to citizens.

Here the most significant challenge and opportunity are coming up with a design solution that not only makes city smart but also makes it sustainable.

The below figure depicts a pictorial representation of the role of a designer and design team in crafting a Smart and Sustainable City.

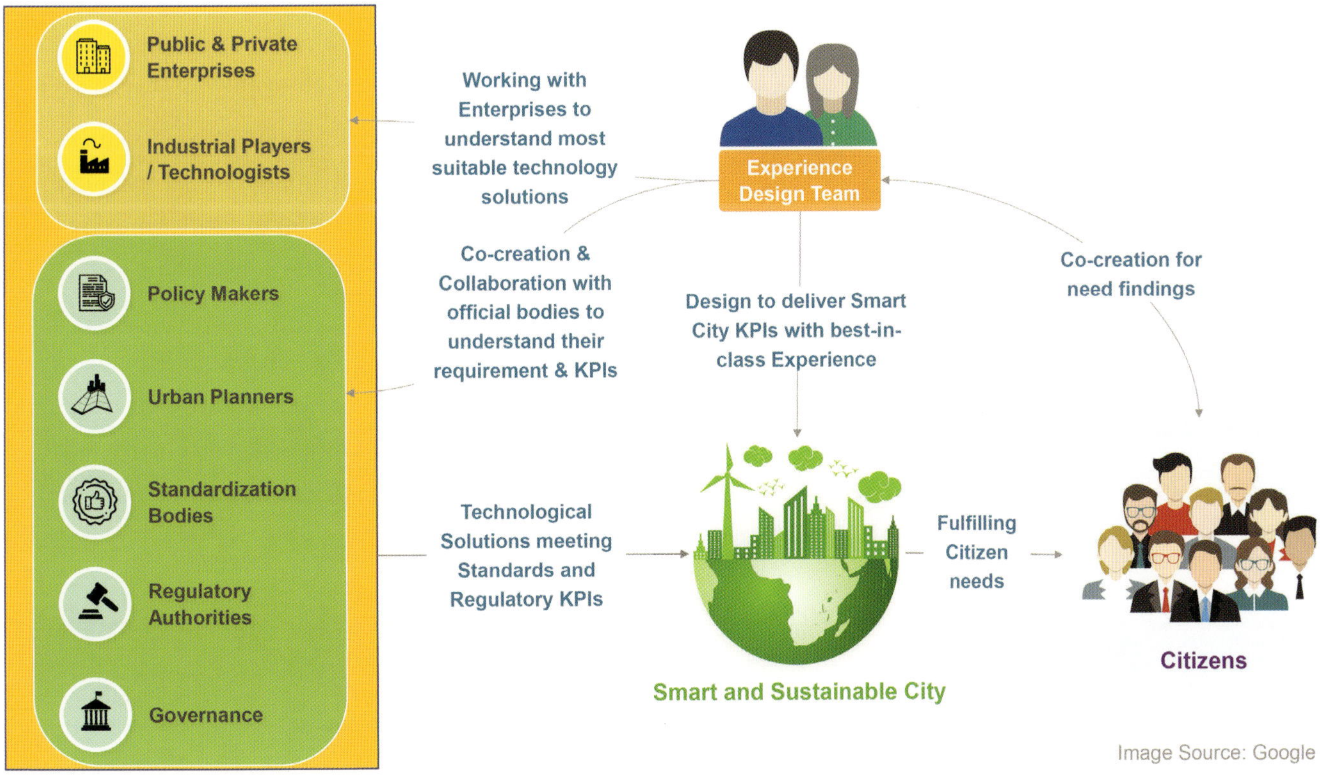

Image Source: Google

The designer and design team have a differentiated role, responsibility, and influence when working with various stakeholders. As designing a Smart City is a multi-competency design effort, a team of vivid expertise is required here, so a diversified group of experts covering not only the design expertise but also the team needs experts from various backgrounds.

Design Team constitutes;

- Various design competencies
- Local culture aspects
- Social awareness
- Human science

As consumers of the Smart City, the design team as a whole and also each member of the group can provide their inputs as well as verify and validate the overall requirements of the Smart City. It is depicted as the 'I' aspect of the influence in the below diagram.

Whereas being part of any entity (e.g., working with regulatory authorities or public and private enterprises, etc.) involved in creating the Smart City, the design team influences the engagement at various levels as the 'We' in the below picture.

Finally, as part of the combined forces, e.g., along with officials and technologies, designers also have an excellent opportunity to influence in crafting best in class Smart City. It is depicted as the 'Us' in the below picture.

So, with this, the role and responsibility of a design team is vast and humongous in coming with a successful Smart City.

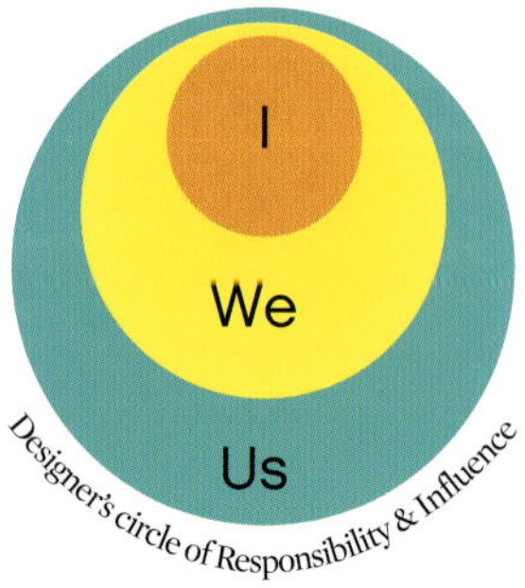

Here designers alongwith various and relevant stakeholders help in setting equity and balanced goals as a new philosophy and a new approach to adopt in urban context development.

4.0 International Best Practices

a) Dubai

'Dubai, the Happiest City on Earth' is the vision of the ruler for Dubai as a Smart City.

Smart Dubai initiative is recreating everyday experiences for residents and visitors of Dubai, making them more personalized, seamless, efficient and impactful by leveraging emerging technologies such as Blockchain and Artificial Intelligence, along with harnessing Data Science capabilities.

Smart Dubai: The government office selected to drive Dubai's citywide transformation into a Smart City, announcing the Smart Dubai Platform, a digital backbone powering the city in the near future, in partnership with the strategic partner Du Telecom Company. The Smart Dubai Platform will be the central operating system for the city, providing access to city services and data for all individuals, the private sector as well as public sector entities. The Smart Dubai Platform is a unique undertaking for any city in the world.

Several leading cities have established ICT platforms but often limited them to specific uses or a single dimension. The newly-conceived Smart Dubai Platform unites city services, IoT, cloud services, Big Data, and digital identity across all city dimensions to build the most comprehensive exchange point for government and private sector services, delivering unprecedented value for the city. The Smart Dubai Platform will be developed with an ambitious and unique public-private partnership model that will set new benchmarks for cross-sector partnerships for smart city initiatives globally.

Smart Dubai is the first Smart City initiative based on the UN's 2030 agenda of Sustainability Development Goals. Smart Dubai Office has launched over 130 initiatives in partnership with government and private sector entities. Some key initiatives include the Dubai Data Initiative, the Dubai Blockchain Strategy, the Happiness Agenda, the Dubai AI Roadmap, and the Dubai Paperless Strategy. Smart Dubai 2021 is a collaboratively-built strategic roadmap for the city to achieve its digital transformation goals by 2021. The roadmap defines ambitious targets across three impact axes: customer happiness, economic growth, and resource and infrastructure resilience.

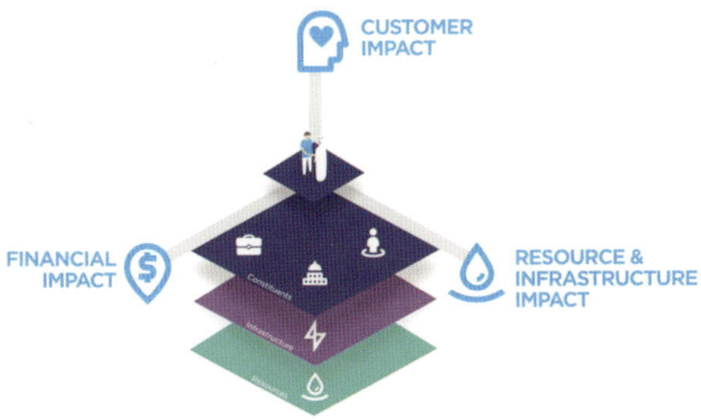

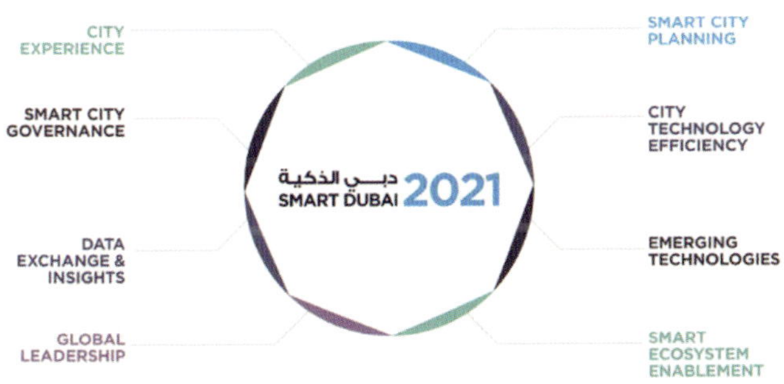

Source: https://2021.smartdubai.ae/

The Office of Smart City Impact Management (OSCIM) has established a full-fledged set of strategic capabilities to oversee and monitor the execution of smart city strategy, which is a large scale, system-wide, a multi-actor transformational effort to make Dubai the happiest city on earth.

b) Singapore

Singapore's ambitious Smart Nation initiative is about harnessing technology to stay ahead as a global city and to improve lives and livelihoods for all.

Through the Smart Nation initiative, we aim to make Singapore "an outstanding city in the world...for people to live, work, and play in, where the human spirit flourishes." To achieve this, we have to apply technology systematically and extensively, rather than in a piecemeal manner, to improve the lives of our people. – Lee Hsien Loong, Prime Minister of Singapore at Smart Nation Launch, 24 November 2014.

In October 2015, almost one year after the launch of the Smart Nation initiative, Singapore became the second city to collaborate with ITU on a two-year pilot project to evaluate the feasibility of specific KPIs for Smart Sustainable Cities.

Singapore is currently one of the many cities around the world that is assessing the efficiency and sustainability of its public services using the KPIs developed by ITU. The Smart Nation framework and the Digital Governance Blueprint and KPIs are as shown below:

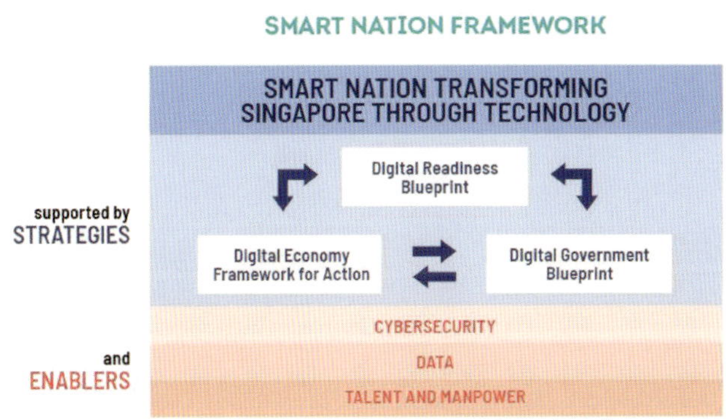

Source: https://www.csc.gov.sg

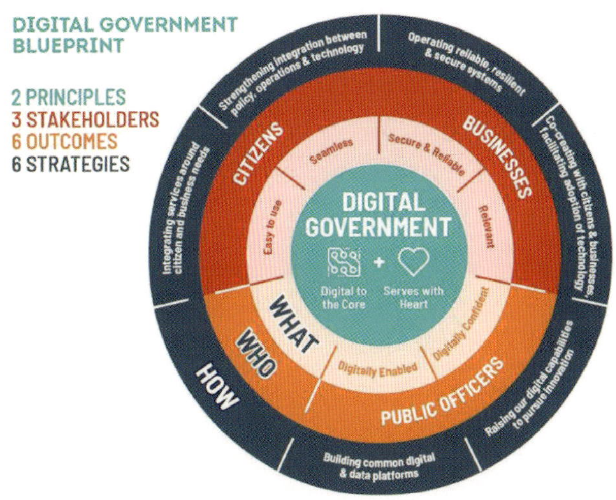

Source: https://www.csc.gov.sg

DIGITAL GOVERNMENT BLUEPRINT KPIS

Area	KPI	Target
STAKEHOLDER SATISFACTION	Citizen Satisfaction with Digital Services (via survey)	75-80% to rate very satisfied
	Business Satisfaction with Digital Services (via survey)	75-80% to rate very satisfied
END-TO-END DIGITAL OPTIONS	Services that offer e-payment options (inbound and outbound)	100%
	Services that are prefilled with Government-verified data	100%
	Services that offer digital options for wet ink signatures	100%*
END-TO-END DIGITAL TRANSACTIONS	Percentage of transactions completed digitally from end-to-end	90-95%*
	Percentage of payments (inbound and outbound) completed via e-payments	100%*
DIGITAL CAPABILITIES	Number of public officers trained in data analytics and data science	20,000
	Number of public officers with basic digital literacy	***All*** Public Officers
TRANSFORMATIVE DIGITAL PROJECTS	Number of transformative digital projects	***30-50*** over a period of 5 years
AI, DATA AND DATA ANALYTICS	Percentage of Ministry families that use AI for service delivery or policy making	***All*** Ministry families to have at least one AI project
	Number of high-impact data analytics projects	***10 cross-agency projects*** per year, and ***2 projects*** per Ministry family per year
	Core data fields in machine readable format, and transmittable by APIs	90-100%
	Time required to fuse data for cross-agency projects	***Less than 10 days*** to share data for cross-agency projects

* Excludes services or individuals where the KPI cannot be met for valid reasons. These reasons can include legislative reasons, or that certain segments of our population (e.g. the elderly or persons with disabilities) are unable to have access to or use digital tools.

Source: https://www.csc.gov.sg

5.0 Expected Outcome

The biggest challenge in the 21st century is knowing how to leverage the benefit of the new generation and upcoming technologies, especially when technology is getting cheaper day-by-day with increased accessibility.

Deploying technology without the right mode of execution plan may not fulfill the citizens' requirements to the fullest. It is where the designers/design team comes into the picture in defining the right and optimal way to cater to the citizens' needs.

Starting with proposal drafting to final solution systems deployment, designers play a considerable role, even though the technical solutions are the problem-solvers; still, the designers plan a significant role in defining, designing, and mode technological solutions.

In short;
"Designers' prime responsibility is to make technologies work for humans to deliver positive experiences."

In both the strategic components of the Smart Cities Mission, area-based development, and pan-city development initiatives, designers have a role to play.

On similar lines, we already see the traces of best practice sharing. For example, Smart Dubai Launches 'Designing Cities' training program 2019 in Tokyo, starting in November 2019.

Acknowledgments

The Confederation of Indian Industry (CII) would like to thank Mr Deep Kapuria, Chairman, CII National Committee on Design and the members of CII National Committee on Design for their encouragement and guidance in bringing about this landmark publication about contemporary Indian design.

We thank the design agencies and industry members for contributing their excellent work with us, which actually make this book a collectors' item.

Confederation of Indian Industry

The Confederation of Indian Industry (CII) works to create and sustain an environment conducive to the development of India, partnering industry, Government, and civil society, through advisory and consultative processes.

CII is a non-government, not-for-profit, industry-led and industry-managed organization, playing a proactive role in India's development process. Founded in 1895, India's premier business association has more than 9100 members, from the private as well as public sectors, including SMEs and MNCs, and an indirect membership of over 300,000 enterprises from 291 national and regional sectoral industry bodies.

CII charts change by working closely with Government on policy issues, interfacing with thought leaders, and enhancing efficiency, competitiveness and business opportunities for industry through a range of specialized services and strategic global linkages. It also provides a platform for consensus-building and networking on key issues.

Extending its agenda beyond business, CII assists industry to identify and execute corporate citizenship programmes. Partnerships with civil society organizations carry forward corporate initiatives for integrated and inclusive development across diverse domains including affirmative action, healthcare, education, livelihood, diversity management, skill development, empowerment of women, and water, to name a few.

India is now set to become a US$ 5 trillion economy in the next five years and Indian industry will remain the principal growth engine for achieving this target. With the theme for 2019-20 as 'Competitiveness of India Inc - India@75: Forging Ahead', CII will focus on five priority areas which would enable the country to stay on a solid growth track. These are - employment generation, rural-urban connect, energy security, environmental sustainability and governance.

With 68 offices, including 9 Centres of Excellence, in India, and 11 overseas offices in Australia, China, Egypt, France, Germany, Indonesia, Singapore, South Africa, UAE, UK, and USA, as well as institutional partnerships with 394 counterpart organizations in 133 countries, CII serves as a reference point for Indian industry and the international business community.

Confederation of Indian Industry

The Mantosh Sondhi Centre,

23, Institutional Area, Lodi Road, New Delhi – 110 003 (India)

T: 91 11 45771000 / 24629994-7 • F: 91 11 24626149

E: info@cii.in • W: www.cii.in

Follow us on: cii.in/facebook cii.in/twitter cii.in/linkedin cii.in/youtube

Reach us via our Membership Helpline: 00-91-124-4592966 / 00-91-99104 46244

CII Helpline Toll Free Number: 1800-103-1244